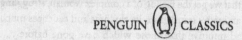

PENGUIN CLASSICS

I, LALLA

RANJIT HOSKOTE is a poet, cultural theorist and curator. His collections of poetry include *Vanishing Acts: New & Selected Poems 1985–2005* (Penguin, 2006) and *Die Ankunft der Vögel* (Carl Hanser Verlag, 2006). His poems have appeared in *Akzente, Boulevard Magenta, Fulcrum, Green Integer Review, Iowa Review, Nthposition* and *Wespennest*. Hoskote was a Fellow of the International Writing Program, University of Iowa (1995), writer-in-residence at Villa Waldberta, Munich (2003), and research scholar in residence at BAK/ basis voor actuele kunst, Utrecht (2010 and 2013).

PRAISE FOR THE BOOK

'Hoskote's success is that we get the feeling of a complex woman, struggling with her times. It is an earthy translation, its rhythms and cadences much more imaginative and intuitive than those which have gone before . . . This is a book to have and to hold. It is beautiful because it is respectful. It is a great translation because the originals have given way to new meanings'—*Hindustan Times*

'With its fine balance between scholarship and creative rigour, Hoskote's book is a persuasive reminder that critical intelligence is not incompatible with the quest for the sacred. This connectedness, Lalla—as ecstatic mystic and discerning guide—reminds us, finds ways to endure, through historical adversity and human amnesia'—*Tehelka*

'Meticulously researched and beautifully written, the book starts with a 69-page introduction which explains the social, historical and philosophical context of Lalla's poems. For the uninitiated, it gives a grounding of the poetic and spiritual legacy of Lal Ded. And for others it unearths the hidden meanings of Lalla's Vakhs . . . When it comes to rendering Lalla's words in English, he does an excellent job. No stilted language, no vague phrases and no attempts to temper with the true spirit of the poems for making it more accessible to the Western readers'—*The Hindu*

'Hoskote's pithy and evocative translation does more than any previous efforts to reduce the semantic gap between Lalla's world and ours'—*Rain Taxi Review of Books*

'Read Hoskote's accomplished translation for the sheer power and colloquial vibrancy with which he retrieves Lalla from the verbosity of Victorian-inflected translations'—*Mint*

'Hoskote's translations are unadorned and distilled down to the essence . . . Lal Ded's poetry is as timeless and as perfect as the beauty of Kashmir. It reflects the latent yearnings that exist in all seekers'—*Times of India, Crest edition*

'Hoskote's translations certainly pose a challenge, inflected as they are with deep scholarship and political awareness'—*Sunday Guardian*

'Poet Ranjit Hoskote's new translation restores the colloquial power of her verse, refreshingly different from earlier ornate paraphrases'—*Indian Express*

'[It] beautifully presents Lalla's writings for what they truly are, and Lalla for what she was—or rather, the different forms that she holds'—*Financial Chronicle*

I, LALLA

The Poems of Lal Děd

Translated from the Kashmiri with
an Introduction and Notes by
RANJIT HOSKOTE

PENGUIN BOOKS
An imprint of Penguin Random House

PENGUIN BOOKS

USA | Canada | UK | Ireland | Australia
New Zealand | India | South Africa | China | Singapore

Penguin Books is part of the Penguin Random House group of companies
whose addresses can be found at global.penguinrandomhouse.com

Published by Penguin Random House India Pvt. Ltd
4th Floor, Capital Tower 1, MG Road,
Gurugram 122 002, Haryana, India

Penguin
Random House
India

First published by Penguin Books India 2011
This paperback edition published in Penguin Books 2013

Copyright © Ranjit Hoskote 2011

10 9 8 7 6 5 4 3 2

ISBN 9780143420781

Typeset in Joanna MT by Eleven Arts, New Delhi
Printed at Manipal Technologies Limited, India

www.penguin.co.in

For *Amma* and *Annu*,
who raised me in the traditions
of the Kashmiri diaspora

Contents

Introduction

1. Lal Děd: Life, Poetry and Historical Context

I didn't believe in it for a moment
but I gulped down the wine of my own voice.
And then I wrestled with the darkness inside me,
knocked it down, clawed at it, ripped it to shreds.

(POEM 48)

The poems of the fourteenth-century Kashmiri mystic Lal Děd strike us like brief and blinding bursts of light: epiphanic, provocative, they shuttle between the vulnerability of doubt and the assurance of an insight gained through resilience and reflection. These poems are as likely to demand that the Divine reveal Itself, as to complain of Its bewildering and protean ubiquity. They prize clarity of self-knowledge above both the ritualist's mastery of observances and the ascetic's professional athleticism. If they scoff at the scholar who substitutes experience with scripture and the priest who cages his God in a routine of prayers, they also reject the renouncer's austere mortification of the body. Across the expanse of her poetry, the author whose signature these poems carry evolves from a wanderer, uncertain of herself and looking for anchorage in a potentially hostile landscape, into a questor who has found belonging beneath a sky that is continuous with her mind.

To the outer world, Lal Dĕd is arguably Kashmir's best known spiritual and literary figure; within Kashmir, she has been venerated both by Hindus and Muslims for nearly seven centuries. For most of that period, she has successfully eluded the proprietorial claims of religious monopolists. Since the late 1980s, however, Kashmir's confluential culture has frayed thin under the pressure of a prolonged conflict to which transnational terrorism, State repression and local militancy have all contributed. Religious identities in the region have become harder and more sharp-edged, following a substantial exodus of the Hindu minority during the early 1990s, and a gradual effort to replace Kashmir's unique and syncretically nuanced tradition of Islam with a more Arabocentric global template. It is true that Lal Dĕd was constructed differently by each community, but she was simultaneously Lalleśvarī or Lalla Yogini to the Hindus and Lal-'ārifa to the Muslims; today, unfortunately, these descriptions are increasingly being promoted at the expense of one another. In honour of the plural sensibilities that Kashmir has long nurtured, I will refer to this mystic-poet by her most celebrated and non-sectarian appellation, 'Lal Dĕd'. In the colloquial, this means 'Grandmother Lal'; more literally, it means 'Lal the Womb', a designation that connects her to the mother goddesses whose cults of fecundity and abundance form the deep substratum of Indic religious life. In writing of her in this book, I will also use the name by which she is most popularly and affectionately known, across community lines: Lalla.

Called *vākhs*, Lalla's poems are among the earliest known manifestations of Kashmiri literature, and record the moment when Kashmiri began to emerge, as a modern language, from the Sanskrit-descended Apabhramśa-prakrit that had been the common language of the region through the first millennium CE. The word *vākh*, applicable both as singular and plural, is cognate with the Sanskrit *vāc*, 'speech', and *vākya*, 'sentence'. This has prompted previous translators to render it as 'saying', 'verse' and 'verse-teaching'; I would prefer to translate it as 'utterance'. A total of 258 *vākhs* attributed to Lalla have circulated widely and continuously in Kashmiri popular culture between the mid-fourteenth century and the present, variously assuming the form of songs, proverbs and prayers.

As we have received them, Lalla's *vākhs* bear the definite imprint of an ongoing process of linguistic and cultural change, which is recorded at the level of form, imagery, concept and vocabulary. Some archaic words and phrases remain embedded in these poems, clues attesting to an earlier stratum of the Kashmiri language; some allegorical references may seem arcane on a first reading, their frames lost to view. We find Sanskritic terms and phrases here, drawn from a larger Hindu-Buddhist universe of meaning that extended from Balkh in the west, across Kashmir, Ladakh and Tibet, to China, Korea and Japan in the east, and southward through the Gangetic regions to peninsular India, Sri Lanka and South-east Asia. These Sanskritic elements share conceptual and linguistic space, in the *vākhs*, with more Arabic or Persianate locutions, indicative of dialogue with the Islamic ecumene that stretched, during Lalla's lifetime, from Spain across North Africa and West Asia to China. Accordingly, we find occasional but unmistakeable hints of Sufi and possibly also of Sikh usage in this corpus of poems. And yet, much of Lalla's poetry is accessible to the contemporary Kashmiri listener or reader, stabilised in the idiom of the late nineteenth and early twentieth centuries: compelling evidence that this oral archive has been updated from generation to generation. Clearly, Lalla's poetry has been continuously read and shared by various assemblies of reciters, scribes and votaries during the nearly seven hundred years of its existence, and has been reshaped and enriched by what we might describe as the informal editorial attention of these assemblies. I shall amplify on this observation in the course of this essay.

As a corpus, the vākhs were first committed to print early in the twentieth century, and have since appeared in several editions, both in the original and in English translation. The line of transmission by which Lalla's poems achieved publication may be traced as a three-stage relay. It begins in the realm of the oral, with the text of the vākhs being woven by various Kashmiri village reciters, Hindu and Muslim, using Kashmiri in a space of relative freedom and play. These demotic recitations dramatise Lalla's importance as an incarnation of compassion, commonsense knowledge and resistance to authority. The relay then passes to the realm of the scribal with the oral text being subordinated to the more annotative and hieratic approach of Kashmiri Brahmin compilers and commentators who, using Sanskrit and Hindi, emphasise Lalla's philosophical convictions and draw traditional moral conclusions from her often unorthodox teachings. The relay culminates in the realm of print, when the scribal text is codified and formatted within the protocols of modern scholarship by compilers and editors: at first by the colonial scholar-administrator using English, followed by South Asian scholars using English, Kashmiri, Urdu and Hindi. In this third stage, the text is stabilised by the fixity of print, and this stability is soon reinforced by the editorial and interpretative scrutiny brought to bear upon the printed text by such modern discursive practices as literary taxonomy, comparative philosophy and religion, Indology and cultural anthropology.

The advent of print generated its own politics in late-colonial societies, where several visions of the nation, society and history were in conflict. Where previously numerous versions of a text had been freely and simultaneously available, printing technology eclipsed these with a single edition consecrated by the authoritative touch of modernity, and which, by bringing all the versions and variants together, transformed simultaneity into competition. In the case of Lalla's *vākhs*, it is significant that the printed text has encoded many of the fluctuations and ambiguities of the transmission line. The availability of such a contestable printed text from late-colonial times always carries the potential for a rivalry of claims to be exercised in the postcolonial period. With regard to Lalla's poems, that potential has been actualised during the political and cultural crisis that erupted in Kashmir in 1989 and continues to the present day. To the extent that Lalla embodies a Kashmiri identity (if not 'the Kashmiri identity'), a piquant battle has been fought around her by various claimants, under the banners of authenticity and historicity.[1] I will address these issues later in this Introduction. Before we continue, it would be appropriate to offer a brief survey of the history and sources of the text of Lalla's poems, as we have it today.

*

In 1914, Sir George Grierson, a scholar, ethnographer and civil servant who had become the first Superintendent of the Linguistic Survey of India on its foundation in 1898, asked his friend and former colleague, Pandit Mukunda Rāma Śastri, to locate a

manuscript of Lalla's poems. Failing to find a copy, Śastri consulted
Pandit Dharma-dāsa Darwēsh, an ageing storyteller and reciter
who lived in Gush, a village situated near the shrine of Śāradā-
pītha, now in Pakistan-occupied Kashmir. Darwēsh dictated 109 of
Lalla's poems from memory and Śastri wrote them down. Adding
a commentary, composed in Hindi and Sanskrit, he sent Grierson
the manuscript. Grierson compared it against two Kashmiri
manuscripts, written in the Śāradā script, which belonged to the
Oxford Indian Institute and formed part of a collection built up
by the legendary Hungarian-British explorer and scholar Sir Marc
Aurel Stein. The first manuscript, or Stein A, is only a fragment of
fifteen leaves; but it is a valuable record of the text of forty-three
of Lalla's poems, with corresponding translations into Sanskrit
verse by a Brahmin redactor, Pandit Rājānaka Bhāskara. The
second manuscript, or Stein B, is of even greater value: it contains
the Kashmiri text of forty-nine of Lalla's poems, offering variant
readings and carrying accentual markings for most of the poems,
to indicate the prosody of the vākhs. Grierson also trawled through
the *Dictionary of Kashmiri Proverbs and Sayings* (1885), compiled by the
Rev. J. Hinton Knowles, a missionary and folklorist working in
Kashmir, and retrieved from this publication a number of sayings
popularly attributed to Lalla.

Collating these materials—together with annotations,
appendices on language, prosody and history, and notes on Yoga
and Kashmir Śaivism by Lionel D. Barnett—Grierson published
the first English translation of Lalla's poems, under the title *Lallā-
Vākyāni, or The Wise Sayings of Lal Ded, A Mystic Poetess of Ancient Kashmir*
(1920). This was also the first printed edition of Lalla's poems
in history. A number of translations have followed Grierson and
Barnett's edition, most notably those of Pandit Ananda Koul

(1921–1933), Sir Richard Carnac Temple (1924), and Professor Jayalal Kaul (1973). More recently, Coleman Barks (1992) has published a rather free literary reworking of Lalla's poems, while Jaishree Kak (1999 and 2007) has published a translation with scholarly exegesis. These, as well as other less widely distributed translations and studies of Lalla's poems, have been enumerated in the References included in this volume.

For the present edition, I have selected 146 poems from the circulating corpus of Lalla's utterances and rendered them freshly into English. My selection includes all 109 of the Grierson and Barnett poems; thirty-four poems that appear in Jayalal Kaul, but not in Grierson and Barnett; and three poems that appear only in Hinton Knowles' *Kashmiri Proverbs*. A concordance, which I have incorporated into my Notes, indicates the textual source of each poem.

*

Paradoxically, given Lalla's pervasive presence in Kashmiri culture, it is difficult to construct a biography for her in the conventional sense. All that we know of her life has been communicated orally, through the medium of legend; the skeletal chronology that we possess is derived from Persian chronicles written in the eighteenth century, nearly four centuries after her death. Although Kashmiri historians produced numerous records of their country's recent past between the fifteenth and seventeenth centuries—this roster includes Jonarāja, Śrīvara, Prājyabhatta, Shuka, Haider Malik Chadura, Tahir and Hasan bin Ali Kashmiri—none of them mentions Lalla. These men concerned themselves with the documentation of dynastic fortunes and shifting political alliances; with accounts of the economy and the climate; with the transformation of religious life through political change. Meanwhile, beneath the line of visibility set by the patriarchy, Lalla's utterances were weaving themselves into Kashmir's popular consciousness.

Lalla is first mentioned in the *Tadhkirāt ul-Ārifīn* (1587), a hagiographic account of saintly figures active in the Valley of Kashmir, written by Mulla Ali Raina, the brother of Srinagar's beloved saint, Makhdum Sahib. This was followed, sixty-seven years later, by a reference in Baba Daud Mishkati's *Asrār ul-Akbar* (1654). Mishkati applies the name 'Lalla' to a yogini who meets a Sultan's son in a forest and offers him a cup, symbolising initiation into the Tantric mysteries; this possibly fabular encounter is borrowed from an episode in Jonarāja's history, where the yogini remains unnamed. Eight decades were to pass before a more plausible and detailed account of Lalla's life appeared in Khwaja Azam Diddamari's *Tārikh-i Āzami* or *Wāqi'āt-i Kashmir* (1736).

We cannot be certain of the date and place of Lalla's birth, or the date and place of her death. Sifting through the evidence of the legends and the chronicles, modern scholars have suggested that she was born in 1301 or between 1317 and 1320, either in Sempore near Pampore, or in Pandrenthan near Srinagar. She is believed to have died in 1373, although no one is certain where; the grave ascribed to her in Bijbehara appears to be of much later provenance. The details of her early life have crystallised into an archetypal narrative of the misunderstood young woman with spiritual aspirations. Born to a Brahmin family, she was married at the age of twelve, as was the custom, into a family that lived in Pampore; she was given a new name, Padmāvati, but remained Lalla in her own eyes. Her domestic life was a troubled one. Suspicious of her meditative absorptions and visits to shrines, her husband treated her cruelly; her mother-in-law often starved her. From this period in Lalla's life comes the well-known Kashmiri saying attributed to the future mystic: 'Whether they kill a ram or a sheep, Lalla will get a stone to eat.'

At twenty-six, Lalla renounced home and family, and went to the Śaiva saint Sĕd Bôyu, or Siddha Śrīkāntha, asking to be accepted as a disciple. He became her guru and instructed her in the spiritual path. On completing her period of discipleship and being initiated, she went out into the world, in the mould of the classical *parivrājikā*, as a wandering mendicant. It is assumed that Lalla began to compose her scintillating, provocative and compelling poems at this stage in her life. To renounce the state of marriage, to wander, gathering spiritual experience: this was not an easy choice for a Brahmin woman to make in the Kashmir of the fourteenth century. As a disciple, she had been secure within her guru's protection; her true ordeals began only after she had left her guru's house and set off on her own, with no armour against the full force of social sanction. As she says in poem 92:

> They lash me with insults, serenade me with curses.
> Their barking means nothing to me.
> Even if they came with soul-flowers to offer,
> I couldn't care less. Untouched, I move on.

Braving the trials and humiliations that came her way, Lalla grew in stature to become a questor and a teacher: this passage to maturity and deepening knowledge is recorded vividly in her *vākhs*. In poem 93, she defies her tormentors and the system of conventions they represent:

Let them hurl a thousand curses at me,
pain finds no purchase in my heart.
I belong to Shiva. Can a scatter of ashes
ruin a mirror? It gleams.

In the specific cultural context of Kashmir, I find instructive
the distinguished sociologist T.N. Madan's comments about the
scepticism expressed by Kashmiri Pandit householders towards
renouncers. Although his informants were mid-twentieth-century
villagers, Madan notes that texts written between the ninth and
the thirteenth centuries confirm a continuity of attitude.

> Why is it that the Pandits distrust and ridicule self-styled
> renouncers? [The answer lies] in their commitment
> to the ideology of the householder. Apparently they
> are cynical about those who leave home because most
> such people never had families of their own . . . or
> their relations with their kin have been strained. At a
> deeper level, however, one might detect a fear of the
> renouncer, for he poses a threat to the ideology of the
> householder and plenitude . . . he not only seeks release
> from the web of kinship and other worldly ties but also
> denigrates these as a trap and an illusion. The renouncer
> is too powerful an adversary to be contemplated with
> equanimity. (1988, 41–42)

Significantly, while many Hindu ascetics had traditionally lived
in the forests of Kashmir, none of Lalla's male predecessors
in the Kashmir Śaiva lineage had been renouncers. They were
scholars, teachers and writers who lived as householders, even

the unmarried among them. Lalla's position was thus a peculiarly paradoxical one. In an ethos where male Śaiva questors lived within society rather than in retreat from it, she could not, as a woman, do likewise. Precisely because she was a woman, whose life was far more closely and rigidly governed by domestic duties and expectations than a man's, she could not lead a life of spiritual aspiration at home—and so, was forced to leave it. Not until the mid-seventeenth century do we find a Kashmiri Brahmin woman saint-poet who received the approval of her family and community for her spiritual quest: Rupa Bhavani (1625–1721), who was clearly a beneficiary of the conceptual space and social legitimation that Lalla had won for her heirs in future generations.

*

Lalla's poems shimmer with their author's experience of being a yogini, trained in the demanding spiritual disciplines and devotional practices of Kashmir Śaivite mysticism. Since this school is itself the confluential outcome of an engagement with several philosophical traditions, she was receptive to the images and ideas of those other traditions. It would be most productive to view her as a figure whose ideas straddled the domains of Kashmir Śaivism, Tantra, Yoga and Yogācāra Buddhism, and who appears to have been socially acquainted with the ideas and practices of the Sufis.

Revelation comes to Lalla like a moon flowering in dark water. Her symbols and allegories can be cryptic, and yet the candour of her poems moves us deeply, viscerally. She celebrates perseverance in the quest, contrasting physical agony with spiritual flight and dwelling on the obdurate landscapes that the questor must negotiate. Lalla's poetry is fortified by a palpable, first-hand experience of illumination; it conveys a freedom from the mortal freight of fear and vacillation. She cherishes these, while attacking the parasitic forms of organised religion that have attached themselves to the spiritual quest and choked it: arid scholarship, soulless ritualism, fetishised austerity and animal sacrifice. Her ways of transcending these obstacles can seem subversive, even deeply transgressive—as in poem 59, where she confronts the priest with the brutal exaction demanded by his idolatry:

> It covers your shame, keeps you from shivering.
> Grass and water are all the food it asks.
> Who taught you, priest-man,
> to feed this breathing thing to your thing of stone?

Kashmir Śaivism recommends the transmutation of all outward observances into visualisations and experiments in consciousness, so that the idol is replaced by the mental image and the sacrifice of an animal by the deliberate extinction of the lower appetites. In this spirit, in poem 61, Lalla rejects the conventional physical elements of worship in favour of meditative depth:

> Kusha grass, flowers, sesame seed, lamp, water:
> it's just another list for someone who's listened,
> really listened, to his teacher. Every day he sinks deeper
> into Shambhu, frees himself from the trap
> of action and reaction. He will not suffer birth again.

At the same time, Lalla asserts the primacy of the guru—regarded as an embodiment of the Divine—as a guide navigating the aspirant through the maze of worldly life towards the central and transfiguring experience of enlightenment. In poem 108, she sings:

Who trusts his Master's word
and controls the mind-horse
with the reins of wisdom,
he shall not die, he shall not be killed.

In yet other poems, she transmits the teachings that are the fruit of her experience: these poems aim to renew the immediacy of everyday life by placing it in the context of eternity, to redeem the self from the cocoon of narcissism and release it towards others, the world and the Divine. In poem 105, she imagines the Divine as a net that traps the individual from within, grace moving by stealth, to be valued in this life rather than deferred as a reward on offer in the afterlife:

The Lord has spread the subtle net of Himself across
the world.
See how He gets under your skin, inside your bones.
If you can't see Him while you're alive,
don't expect a special vision once you're dead.

In consonance with Kashmir Śaiva doctrine, Lalla regards the world as an array of traps for the unwary, so long as the self remains amnesiac towards its true nature. On realising that the world is the playful expression of the Divine, and that the Divine and the self are one, anguish and alienation fall away from the consciousness, to be replaced by the joyful recognition that all dualisms are illusory. This leads her to rejoice in the collapse of such restrictive identities as 'I' and 'You' when confronted with the presence of the Divine, as in poem 15:

> Wrapped up in Yourself, You hid from me.
> All day I looked for You
> and when I found You hiding inside me,
> I ran wild, playing now me, now You.

Lalla enacts the theatre of her devotion in different registers. She yearns, she demands, she laments; she can be prickly and irritable with the Divine, yet throw herself at Its mercy and sing of unabashed passion, as in poem 47:

> As the moonlight faded, I called out to the madwoman,
> eased her pain with the love of God.
> 'It's Lalla, it's Lalla,' I cried, waking up the Loved One.
> I mixed with Him and drowned in a crystal lake.

Lalla treats the body as the site of all her experiments in self-refinement: she asserts the unity of the corporeal and the cosmic, as achieved through immersive meditation and the Yogic cultivation of the breath. The subtle channels and nodal points of the Yogic body form a basic reality for her, its terrain as real as the topography of lake, river and mountains that recurs in her compositions. In poem 52, she declares:

I trapped my breath in the bellows of my throat:
a lamp blazed up inside, showed me who I really was.
I crossed the darkness holding fast to that lamp,
scattering its light-seeds around me as I went.

For Lalla, the symbolic and the sensuously palpable are not in opposition, but rather, suffuse one another. The cultural theorist and historian Richard Lannoy interprets this feature of Indic philosophy and spiritual practice elegantly:

Each successive school of philosophy, each mystic, sage, or saint, sought by one means or another to appropriate the external world to the mind-brain. He enhanced, expanded, intensified, and deepened his sensory awareness of colours, sounds, and textures until they were transformed into vibrations continuous with his own consciousness. In this state of enhanced consciousness induced by special techniques of concentration, the inside and the outside, the subject and the object, the self and the world, did not remain separate entities but fused in a single process. (1971, 273–74)

*

For an itinerant, tangential and seemingly isolated dissident—she founded no school or movement, had no apostles, left no anointed successors, and scattered her poems among her listeners—Lalla has exerted a profound and seminal influence on Kashmir's religious life. She was a major presence in the life and practice, not only of Rupa Bhavani, but also of a number of later Kashmiri mystics, teachers and devotional poets like Parmanand (1791–1879), Shams Faqir (1843–1904), and Krishna Joo Razdan (1851–1926). Vitally, given that Kashmir is now almost completely a Muslim region, it is instructive to recall that Lalla is regarded as a foundational figure by the Rishi order of Kashmiri Sufism, which was initiated by Nund Rishi or Sheikh Nur-ud-din Wali (1379–1442), seen by many as her spiritual son and heir. Nur-ud-din and his fellow Rishis chose to lead celibate lives, abstained from meat, avoided injuring animals or plants, secluded themselves in caves or forests, and employed an ecumenical vocabulary drawn both from the Kashmir Śaivite and Islamic systems. The Rishis instituted solitary meditative as well as collective devotional practices, and their followers convene around a network of khānaqahs or ziyārats: shrine complexes that incorporate mosques, meditation halls and the tombs of saints. This robust regional tradition of spirituality continues to remain strong in the Valley, despite the hardening of Islamic piety along Wahhabi mandates during the low-intensity warfare between insurgents and the Indian State that has raged unabated in recent decades, accompanied by cycles of civil unrest and the killing of countless innocent people, Muslim and Hindu, caught in the crossfire.

Lalla, too, lived through a time of seismic turbulence. Between 1320 and 1339, Kashmir suffered a rapid sequence of political catastrophes threaded together by intrigue, conspiracy, crippling incompetence, lust for power and thwarted ambition. The country was attacked by the Tartar chieftain Zulchu, which prompted the downfall of the last Hindu king of Kashmir, Sahadeva, and of his prime minister and legatee, Rāmachandra. Into this vacuum stepped a Tibetan prince from Ladakh, Rinchana, who had

taken refuge at Sahadeva's court some years before. He married
Rāmachandra's daughter, Kotā, and asked to be accepted as a
Śaiva; short-sightedly, the Brahmin priesthood turnèd him down,
and he soon embraced Islam under the tutelage of Sayyid Sharaf-
ud-din or Bulbul Shah, a Sufi from Khorasan who had made his
home in the Valley. When Rinchana died, his widow Kotā made
common cause with Shah Mir, an adventurer from Swat who
had also settled in the Valley; they invited Sahadeva's brother
Udyānadeva to rule. As his brother had done, Udyānadeva too
fled when Kashmir was attacked by the Turki chieftain Achala; he
returned after the raid to find Kotā both popular and dominant,
and was never again more than her puppet. After his death, Kotā
and Shah Mir attempted to outmanoeuvre one another, but the
queen had run out of survivor's luck at last. She killed herself,
leaving Shah Mir as undisputed ruler of Kashmir: he ascended the
throne in 1339 as Sultan Shams-ud-din, the 'Sun of the Faith'.

Shams-ud-din's coronation marks Kashmir's transition from
a Hindu-Buddhist past to a future that would be shaped by the
gradual diffusion of Islam, although Hindus and Buddhists
continued to dominate Kashmiri politics and culture for several
generations longer. The dynasty that Shams-ud-din founded was
to rule Kashmir for two centuries, and Lalla lived through his
reign and those of his son Ala-ud-din and his grandson Shihab-
ud-din. These early sultans gradually brought a measure of peace
and prosperity to the region, and extended their patronage to
the arts and learning. Only much later in the fourteenth century
was their policy of liberalism abrogated briefly by the fanaticism
of Sultan Sikandar. Spurred on by his minister Saif-ud-din, a
Brahmin convert originally called Suha Bhatta, this ruler launched
a programme of persecution, destroying temples and forcing

many Brahmins into exile. Sikandar was an aberration, however, and his son Zain-ul-abedin restored the Sultanate's policy of generosity and inclusiveness, inviting émigré Brahmins back to the Valley and having Sanskrit works translated into Persian (Bamzai 1994, 2:316–28).

*

While surveying the wider context of religious developments in the Indian subcontinent, scholars have sometimes sought to historicise Lalla in relation to the Bhakti movements that swept across this landmass between the fourteenth and the sixteenth centuries. These were popular mobilisations that opposed the hierarchical orthodoxy of Brahminism, regional surges of protest that crystallised around charismatic reformers or renouncers who insisted on the revolutionary idea that a direct and loving communion between the worshipper and the Divine was possible without priestly intermediaries or ritual specialists. The term 'Bhakti' (literally meaning 'devotion') has been used to encompass a spectrum of formations ranging from the northern Sant tradition, including Rāmānanda, Tulsidās, Kabīr, Nānak and Dādu, to the western Vārkari lineage, with Jnāneśvara, Nāmdev and Tukārām as its leading figures. It also connotes several parallel developments, including the rise of the forms of Vaiṣṇava devotionalism associated with Chaitanya in Bengal and Vallabha across northern India, and the consolidation of the Śaivite Lingāyat movement in Karnataka and of the Śrivaiṣṇavas in Tamil Nadu.

The proponents of Bhakti turned their backs on the elaborate structure of worship that was integral to Brahminical practice. Instead, they promoted a deeply felt and richly expressed devotion focused on a chosen embodiment of the Divine. Rejecting Sanskrit, the *deva-bhāśa* or 'language of the gods', they preached and composed their poetry in the *loka-bhāśa* or languages of everyday life that were organic to the regions in which the movements had arisen. This confident vernacularisation of expression, in preference over the epigonic classicism that was the norm among the Brahminical elite, marks the emergence of many modern Indian languages including Kannada, Marathi, Hindi and Bengali. The Bhakti movements developed a mass base among the subaltern and labouring castes—greatly oppressed by the social hierarchies of late mediaeval India—providing them with their first major articulation in history. In many ways, therefore, these movements mark an early and revolutionary threshold of modernity in India.

Some commentators have viewed Lalla as a forerunner of Bhakti, and she certainly anticipated the women saints who were to play an important role in these movements, such as Mīrā and Bahinā, in breaking away from restrictive patriarchal structures. Other observers have sought to subsume Lalla quite completely within the historical momentum of Bhakti, with some university syllabi even enlisting her in the array of Bhakti saint-poets. In my view, this is an error of ahistorical thinking. These Procrustean procedures not only generate a monolithic and *a priori* notion of Bhakti, but they also allow the compelling social and political dimensions of the Bhakti mobilisations to overshadow the fact that *bhakti-mārga*, the way of intense and self-dissolving devotion, is only one among the three major approaches to the Divine recognised in Hindu practice. The others are *karma-mārga*, or adherence to the prescribed ritual forms, and *jnāna-mārga*, or the path of evolved awareness and world-transcending insight.

Many features of Lalla's practice do indeed bear an affinity to Bhakti spirituality, especially her opposition to the religious hierarchy and orthodox worship integral to *karma-mārga*, her sense of direct communion with the Divine, her valorisation of the Name as a talisman, and her use of the language of everyday life. But Lalla's perspective, like the Kashmir Śaiva perspective more generally, is premised far more substantially on *jñāna-mārga* than on *bhakti-mārga*. Lalla is concerned with nurturing a radical transformation of consciousness aimed at recovering the identity of the self with the Divine; she is not chiefly preoccupied with a brimming-over of devotional expression by which the self embraces the Divine. And unlike the Bhakti saint-poets, who lived and worked in communities, the evidence in her poems as well as in the legends and the chronicles suggests that Lalla, while interacting with groups of aspirants, was a figure who walked alone.

2. The Vectors of Lalla's Voice: Single Author or Contributory Lineage?

You've got six and I've got six.
Now tell me, Blue-Throated One, what's the difference?
Or don't. I know. You keep your six on a leash
and my six have strung me along.

(POEM 24)

Since the late 1980s, the study of Lalla's poetry has undergone an unfortunate sectarian polarisation between Kashmiri Pandit and Kashmiri Muslim scholars; these academic groupings hold diametrically opposed visions of Kashmiri culture, literature, religious life and identity. Some of the former claim Lalla exclusively for Kashmir Śaivism and reject any hint of Islamic influence on her beliefs or acquaintance with Sufism on her part, citing as evidence the Yogic symbolism, details of spiritual practices and hints of biography that appear in her *vākhs* (for example, Toshkhani 2002, 39–66). Meanwhile, some of the latter attempt to induct Lalla into Kashmir's early Sufi ethos, arguing that her emancipatory teachings could not have sprung from a Hindu matrix, and pointing out that the earliest references to her occur in Sufi hagiographies and Persian chronicles written by Muslims (for example, Khan 2002, 70–79).

The first position, which I shall call the Śaiva-only school, characterises Islam as an alien import imposed by West and Central Asian missionaries. It chooses to ignore the vibrant confluence between the Yogic and the Sufi traditions of spirituality that had begun to be established through the dialogues between Brahmin and Sufi sages in fourteenth-century Kashmir. Indeed, many members of the Rishi order were Brahmin ascetics who converted to Islam, bringing to it the contemplative flavour of the *sanyāsin*'s life of retreat and prayer. The Śaiva-only school also refuses to credit the density of accounts which suggest that Lalla was held in high esteem by her Sufi contemporaries. Even if several of the more famous of these accounts are either implausible on chronological grounds or are obviously motivated by the requirements of religious propaganda,[2] there must have been some shared grounds of vision and discourse that led the Sufis to embrace Lalla's poetry, and to recite her *vākhs* as invocations while opening their assemblies (see Kak 2007, 3).

The second position, which I shall call the Sufi-only school, presents pre-Islamic Kashmir as a *jahiliyya* or stronghold of paganism awaiting Islam's redemptive touch. It makes formulaic attacks on Kashmir's supposedly degenerate Brahmins—a curious degeneracy, which produced such eloquently non-dualist teachers as Vasugupta, Utpaladeva and Abhinavagupta, who prized illumination above idols. The Sufi-only school also insists that the suffering Kashmiri populace, eager to be rid of the Brahmin ascendancy, accepted Islam with enthusiasm. The historical record shows that the early Sufi missionaries invited only a few key people, not the masses, to convert; mass conversion was achieved because these individuals were followed obediently into Islam by their families and clans. This change of religion did not necessarily involve a deeply realised *metanoia*. As a result, even as late as the sixteenth century, there were complaints about the religious laxity of Kashmir's Muslims, whose Islam was often nominal (see Wani 2007, 13–21).

The partisans on both sides of this dispute downplay or explain away historical evidence that is inconvenient to their positions, which are rooted in the ideological compulsions of the present. Indeed, this dispute over the true nature of Lalla's spirituality, poetry and teachings puts us in mind of the quarrel that is believed to have broken out after Kabīr's death between his Hindu and Muslim followers, the former wishing to cremate and the latter to bury the master's body. When the shroud was pulled away, all they found was a heap of fresh flowers.

*

Authenticity and historicity are the key categories around which this dispute is staged. As we have seen, Lalla's poems were available as an open-ended corpus that was in a state of play until stabilised (or arrested, if you prefer) by print modernity in the early twentieth century; as such, they contain Sanskritised verses on Yogic practice as well as Persianate technical terms for the soul or the Lord, robust accounts of secret Tantric rites as well as pithy words of folk wisdom. In pursuit of the authentic core of poems produced by the historical Lalla, some scholars have become preoccupied with refining away all the materials that they regard as corrupt or as interpolations. The problem with this approach is that there is no mythic Old Kashmiri original to be retrieved; as we have seen, every generation has revised the phrasing of Lalla's poems towards contemporary usage. This leaves observers free to let their ideological preferences dictate their linguistic researches: the Śaiva-only school condemns all Persianate phrasing as insertions made by later Muslim hands; equally, the Sufi-only school could well construe Sanskritic terminology as evidence of later Brahminical imposition.

Meanwhile, even as each school defers to a vague notion of Lalla's 'style', no clear explanation is provided for the enormous variety of registers, tonalities, rhythms and gradations of vocabulary that are accreted within her poetry. Even though Lalla's poems are linked by a metrical structure—typically, each vākh has four lines, and each line has four beats—their music changes constantly. Some of the poems are festive, others melancholic, yet others combative; some spell out a pensive reflection, others open out into a passionate cry from the heart, yet others rap out a quick-step dance measure. Lalla switches style from one poem to the next, and in following her, we realise that while a Perso-Arabic expression would almost certainly have entered the corpus several centuries after Lalla's death, the

Sanskrit phraseology might equally have been inserted by a much later Brahmin scribe or reciter.

Nor can we maintain such a sharp distinction between Muslim and Pandit. Since families and clans in Kashmir have often transited from Hinduism to Islam in the space of a generation or two, it is unlikely that they would have abandoned all their inherited theological reflexes and linguistic habits instantly. During the Sultanate, an administrative language was cobbled together from Sanskrit, Persian and Arabic, and employed to frame land grants, scrips and agreements; it remained in use well into the mid-seventeenth century. Writing as late as 1900, Aurel Stein reported his discovery of Sanskrit inscriptions on Muslim gravestones during his journeys through Kashmir in 1888 and 1896 (see Kalhana 1900, 131). Therefore, it is not impossible that some of the Sanskritic interpolations in Lalla's corpus were made by Muslims. In this connection, let us recall that Nund Rishi or Sheikh Nur-ud-din Wali's poems, known as śruks, from the Sanskrit śloka, are replete with terms such as nirguna and avatāra.

None of this should be surprising. The linguist Braj Kachru proposed the influential model of a Kashmiri bifurcated between 'Sanskritised Kashmiri' and 'Persianised Kashmiri' (Kachru 1969a) to account for styles within the language, which may broadly be mapped onto Pandit and Muslim sociolinguistic usage. And yet it has been pointed out that these are tendencies rather than styles; that the two communities do not use their respective styles exclusively or invariably; and that style switching has historically been common between the two communities, with speakers subtly altering their choice of address, vocabulary and tonal shading in different contexts, depending on their interlocutors (O.N. Koul 1977).

Significantly, even the magisterial Jayalal Kaul insisted that he could not guarantee the authenticity of the 138 *vākhs* that he had chosen from the 258 circulating in Lalla's name, while preparing his 1973 edition. He arrived at this distillate after addressing all extant Lalla editions; he also collected every Lalla poem that he could find among the reciters of the Valley, adding another seventy-five verses to his collection. At the end of this exercise, he filtered out all variants and interpolations. In addition to three quatrains written by Azizullah Khan in the early nineteenth century and attributed to Lalla, he found that thirty-five poems occurred simultaneously in recensions of Lalla's poetry and in the Nur-*namas* and Rishi-*namas*, which record the utterances of Nund Rishi; another three poems appeared both in the Lalla recensions and the *Rahasyopadeśa* of Rupa Bhavani.

In light of this discussion of the probable sources and circumstances of the interpolations in Lalla's poetry, I would propose a radical break with the established convention of treating Lal Děd as a single personality and interpreting her poetry as an account of the vicissitudes of a single life. While affirming that Lalla's poetry is deeply anchored in the personal experiences of an individual who actually lived and suffered, gloried in theophany and crafted a remarkable life in hostile circumstances, I shall argue that the poetry that has come down to us in her name is not the work of an individual. Rather, it has been produced over many centuries by what I would term a contributory lineage, a sequence of assemblies comprising people of varied religious affiliations and of both genders, representing the experience of various age groups and social locations, including both literate and unlettered, reciters and scribes, redactors and commentators.[3]

These assemblies functioned as a living archive networked across the Valley, re-crafting, amplifying and adding to Lalla's poems. Gathering in response to the auratic presence of the historical Lalla, they worked in consonance with what they saw as the core truth of her experienced revelation. In such a collective model of authorship, every contribution is a devotional act, and is therefore offered as an attribution to the saint-poet. This would explain why the vectors of Lalla's voice have remained largely anonymous. In picturing Lalla's poems as the LD corpus, developed by a contributory lineage, I find myself encouraged by Vinay Dharwadker's finely woven account of the fifteenth-century saint-poet Kabīr, whose poetry he views as a complex multi-author production spanning five centuries and mediated through multiple languages, regions and teaching lineages (Dharwadker 2003).

For these reasons, the notion of authenticity is not useful to my model. Authenticity, which demands that we demarcate a pure Ur-text and eliminate all later accretions, is a chimera—whether for literary texts, religions or cultures. This becomes evident when the only true token of Lalla's authorship that we are offered is 'the evidence of diction and prosody, and the quality of cast of thought, the way it is organised in the process of expression, in a word, the characteristic style of Lal Ded' (Jayalal Kaul, in Toshkhani 2002, 121) or, in the same vein, when we are told that 'it is the style of the verses that determines their validity as hers' (Kak 2007, 3). Style, unfortunately, is what an adroit imitator captures best, even to the point of outdoing the original.

I find it far more fruitful to engage with the versionality of the LD corpus, which arises from the participatory nature of the contributory lineage that produced it. Correspondingly, I would identify, but not be agitated by, gestures of interpolation—which I see to be organic to the way in which the corpus has grown between the fourteenth and the twentieth centuries. While some scholars have pointed out later additions to the text in order to purge them, I would point these out for the opposite reason: to celebrate them, in Bakhtin's terms, as evidence of the vibrant *heteroglossia* of the LD corpus, its gift for orchestrating a *polyphony* of variegated tones, registers and voices.[4]

In the present edition, I have included seven *vākhs* that contain Sufi inflections, and commented on them accordingly in the Notes: these are poems 17, 18, 29, 69, 70, 71 and 104. Of these, 17, 18 and 69 are the Azizullah Khan quatrains, and form an important test case for my theory of the contributory lineage. Poems 17 and 18 appear in Grierson and Barnett, sourced from the Pandit Dharma-dāsa Darwēsh recitation: this shows that Azizullah's poems had been seamlessly incorporated into the LD corpus over the nineteenth century, and were presented as Lalla material even by Pandit reciters. A variant that subsumes poems 17 and 18 appears in Knowles, which suggests that Azizullah may have reworked pre-existing material that was available to other contributors as well, or that his contributions were in turn re-edited and recast by others. Contemporary readers familiar with the workings of open-source software would not be astonished by such a process of simultaneous, multi-user editing. Poem 69 appears only in Knowles: I have retained it while annotating it clearly as a later addition; yet, again, can we say for certain that it was not a rephrasing, by Azizullah, of an earlier poem attributed to Lalla? Poem 29 is recorded only by Knowles. The companion poems 70 and 71 appear in Grierson; 70 is also recorded by Kaul. Poem 104 appears only in Kaul.

I hope to have demonstrated the fatuity of attempting to establish a true Lalla, purely Sanskritic or purely Perso-Arabic depending upon our ideological preferences. She is a play of versions, not an absolute entity: to the ear that receives her poems, the body of the *vākh* is the only true Lalla there is. Ultimately, we must ask ourselves what we wish to believe. Does the saint-poet stand before and apart from the text, resident in a biographical persona that scholars construct from scanty data, the texture of rumour and the colour of fable? Or does the saint-poet breathe within the text, through the flow of the poems attributed to her, vigorously and often meticulously produced in her name, and relayed through a popular imagination that had not been overtaken by print modernity or weakened by the manipulations and blandishments of the electronic media? Lalla, to me, is not the person who composed these *vākhs*; rather, she is the person who emerges from these *vākhs*.

3. Lalla's Poetry: Reconstructing its Religious and Philosophical Horizons

Neither You nor I, neither object nor meditation,
just the All-Creator, lost in His dreams.
Some don't get it, but those who do
are carried away on the wave of Him.

(POEM 116)

The Lalla who emerges from the LD corpus is, without any doubt, a Śaiva yogini. Emotionally rich yet philosophically precise, sumptuously enigmatic yet crisply structured, Lalla's poems are shaped within the horizons of Kashmir Śaivism, Yoga and Tantra. The Persianate terms that appear in the LD corpus do not mark the introduction of Islamic concepts into Lalla's thought, but rather, indicate a rendering of her ideas in Sufi phraseology. Such acts of translation would follow naturally in an environment where philosophies were in dialogue, and given that non-dualist Śaivism and monist Sufism have certain specific points of convergence: *mokṣa* and *fan'ā*, *jīvātman* and *naphs*, are not very far apart.

Since Lalla stands at the threshold between an old Hindu-Buddhist Kashmir whose contours have been somewhat blurred in public memory, and a new Islamic Kashmir whose history is far better known, there has been a tendency to present her simply as the forerunner of the Rishi order of Sufism, founded by Sheikh Nur-ud-din Wali, the *ālamdār-i Kashmir* or 'standard-bearer of Kashmir'. As against this, I would argue, as some scholars have done before me, that the historical Lalla could more productively be seen as the inheritor of a long line of brilliant Kashmir Śaivite practitioners and expositors who flourished between the eighth and the eleventh centuries CE, including Vasugupta, Bhatta Nārāyana, Utpaladeva, Lakshmanadeva and Abhinavagupta. Going further, and building here on a model proposed by Richard Lannoy (1971, 168–76) and a suggestion made by the historian Peter Heehs (2002, 293), I would hazard the suggestion that she was a member of what I would describe as a *Tantric underground* spread across the sacred geography of the Indian subcontinent. The evidence suggests that she innovated around the Sanskrit and Apabhramśa teachings of the Śaiva masters and explored the spiritual alchemy of the Tantras. Choosing to compose her utterances in the evolving language of the common people, she injected these powerful currents into the popular consciousness.

The liminal figure, especially if she is a woman who has made heterodox choices, is extremely vulnerable to misrepresentation: Lalla was a wanderer who had deliberately de-classed herself, used the demotic rather than the elite language, and refused to found a new movement or join an established order. Various commentators, including those otherwise well disposed towards her, have proposed the most patronising explanations for Lalla's spiritual attainments, her poetry and her teachings. Some allow her a little acquaintance with Yoga and Tantra; some concede that she knew a little philosophy but imply that she picked it up informally and intuitively; and some doubt that a woman could have gained the sophistication of an initiate. Professor A.N. Dhar writes: 'It is essentially through the *vākhs, which she uttered as direct outpourings from her heart rather than as consciously wrought poetic compositions*, that Lalla became very popular as a saint-poet in Kashmir' (in Toshkhani 2002, 13; emphasis mine). Even Peter Heehs, who contextualises Lalla within the Siddha, Nātha and Yoga traditions, writes that she 'undoubtedly knew something of the teachings of Kashmir Śaivism, though not through Sanskrit texts' (2002: 293). These are baffling attitudes. Why is it so difficult to believe—especially when she says so herself in the most eloquent manner—that, at the core of the LD corpus, there really was a woman mystic who had put herself through the rigours of initiation into Kashmir Śaivism, Tantra and Yoga? As Lalla says in poem 51, recording the awakening of the subtle body through a Yogic technique:

My mind boomed with the sound of Om,
my body was a burning coal.
Six roads brought me to a seventh,
that's how Lalla reached the Field of Light.

*

Our road, as we map the religious and philosophical lifeworld
in which Lalla's poetry emerged, now brings us to Kashmir
Śaivism. The foundations of Śaivite philosophy lie in the
Śaiva-āgāmas or tantras, high among which may be ranked the
Vijñānabhairava (c. 8th century CE), composed in Sanskrit and
developed in northern India between the fourth and eighth
centuries. These were cast as dialogues between Shiva and
Shakti concerning the structure of the cosmos and of human
experience, the pathways to spiritual illumination, and modes
of effecting release from the cycle of birth and death. The
tantras posit a framework of thirty-six cosmic principles, which
culminate in Shiva and Shakti, and beyond this dyad, in the
ineffable and unitive essence of the universe, which is referred
to as Parama-shiva (rendered in the Notes to this translation as
the 'Shiva-principle'). The Śaivite tradition developed through
three major branches: the dualist Śaiva Siddhānta system that
arose in the Tamil country in the sixth century, its texts composed
in Tamil; the non-dualist Kashmir Śaivism that announced
itself in the eighth century, its texts composed in Sanskrit with
Apabhramśa annotations; and the dualist Virasaiva or Lingāyat
movement that exploded in Karnataka in the twelfth century, its
texts composed in Kannada (Heehs 2002, 243–44).

Non-dualist Kashmir Śaivism emerged as a distinctive
philosophy after intensive dialogue with the thousand-year

tradition of Mahāyāna Buddhism, especially the sophisticated epistemology and psychology of its Yogācāra school (also known as the Vijñānavāda), which originated in Gandhara and Kashmir. Kashmir Śaivism also benefited from a confrontation with the newly emergent Vedānta monism of the intellectually energetic Kerala monk and systematiser of modern Hinduism, Śankara. The Kashmir Śaivites concur with the Yogācārins that the phenomenal world is real only to the extent that it is perceived to exist through the medium of the consciousness. Accordingly, a refinement of consciousness leads to a refinement of the understanding of the phenomenal world. To the Yogācārins, as to the Kashmir Śaivites, no objects exist independently of perception, there is really no world outside the self; and indeed, the experiencing self and the experienced world are both products of the processes of cognition and imagination.[5] With the Vedāntins, the Kashmir Śaivites agree that there is only one ultimate reality, and that there is no distinction between the Divine and the human, except through a forgetfulness of one's true nature.

By contrast with both Yogācāra and Vedānta, though, Kashmir Śaivism does not dismiss the world as an illusion or delusion. It treats the world as a creative expression of the Divine, a necessary articulation through which the Divine may unfold and fully realise itself. Shiva, through Shakti, creates a world that is not different from Himself. This world is constantly renewed through the cosmic vibrations or *spanda*—emanations of the Shiva-principle—that, in their outward-expansive and inward-contractive rhythm, *unmeṣa* and *nimeṣa*, define the universal cycle of creation and dissolution. Further, in the Kashmir Śaivite system, the Shiva-principle has a triadic nature, devolving through the world as the three energies of knowledge, will and action:

respectively, jñāna-śakti, icchā-śakti and krīyā-śakti. Sustained by this triadic structure, the world is seen to replicate it at many levels; that is why Kashmir Śaivism is also known as Trika, the 'Path of the Triad'. It is difficult not to hear, in these formulations, an echo of the triadic preferences of the Yogācāra theorists, who propounded the trikāya or 'Doctrine of the Three Bodies of the Buddha' and the corresponding trisvabhāva-nirdeśa or 'Teaching of the Three Natures'.

At the other end of the scale from this vision of the cosmos is the individual soul, which is imprisoned because it has forgotten its true nature and become enmeshed in the net of thought, attachment and the consequences of unreflective action. Once it recognises the continuity between Shiva and the world, both through the appropriate rituals but far more importantly through the insight gained from sustained meditation, the soul can join in the festivity of being, recognising all to be the play or līla of Shiva. That recognition, or pratyabhijñā, is the key transformative experience in Kashmir Śaivite practice: it recurs constantly in Lalla's poetry. As she says in poem 25:

> Lord! I've never known who I really am, or You.
> I threw my love away on this lousy carcass
> and never figured it out: You're me, I'm You.
> All I ever did was doubt: Who am I? Who are You?

The major texts of Kashmir Śaivism include the Śiva Sūtra of Vasugupta (mid-eighth century); the Stava-cintāmani of his disciple, Bhatta Nārāyana, who images Shiva as prakāsha or light, and Shakti as vimarśa or self-awareness; the Spanda literature of the ninth to eleventh centuries; and the writings of Somānanda

(c. 875–925) and Utpaladeva (c. 900–950). This textual tradition peaks in the writings of the encyclopaedic master Abhinavagupta (c. 950–1020) and continues through texts such as Śitikāntha's *Mahānaya-prakāsha* (c. 1250), regarded as the first complete text written in Kashmiri.

The continuity of Lalla's thought with this philosophical lineage is evident, as I shall demonstrate by a few apposite comparisons of her poems with those of her predecessors. Such comparisons reveal the high degree of intertextuality that binds Lalla's texts to those of her predecessors in an active continuum knit together by allusion and the adaptation of ideas and images already in circulation among initiates and adepts. For instance, Utpaladeva writes, in his tenth-century *Śiva-stotra* (translated from the Sanskrit by Constantina Rhodes Bailly; Heehs 2002, 246):

> In that state, O Lord,
> Where nothing else is to be known or done,
> Neither *yoga*
> Nor intellectual understanding
> Is to be sought after,
> For the only thing that remains and flourishes
> Is absolute consciousness.

Recording her experience of the same condition of expanded awareness four hundred years later, Lalla says, in poem 115:

> Word or thought, normal or Absolute, they mean nothing
> here.
> Even the mudrās of silence won't get you entry.

We're beyond even Shiva and Shakti here.
This Beyond that's beyond all we can name, that's
                                    your lesson!

Expounding on the exemplar of the *jīvan-mukta*—the realised soul who is indifferent to living and dying, and who lives in the fullness of enlightenment—the tenth-century aesthetician, literary theorist, yogi and Tantric adept Abhinavagupta, writes in his *Parātrimśikā-vivarana* (adapted from a translation from the Sanskrit by Paul Eduardo Muller-Ortega; Heehs 2002, 248):

> Through the peculiar efficacy of the ritual of adoration—
> by practising which he has remembered perfectly the
> *mantra*, and so attained to a very high degree the potency
> of that *mantra*, which is the reality known as the Heart—the
> tantric practitioner crosses over completely, either by
> himself or as a result of the clear and pristine lotus-word
> of the teacher, and in this way attains liberation in this
> very life.

Lalla, affirming the joyous liberation of the *jīvan-mukta* from the prison of mortal birth four centuries later, says in poem 125:

> Those who glow with the light of the Self
> are freed from life even while they live.
> But fools add knots by the hundred
> to the tangled net of the world.

Abhinavagupta, the most accomplished of the Śaiva *āchāryas*, also composed a beautiful and moving prayer called the

Mahopadeśa-vimśatikam, in the third verse of which he writes (translation from the Sanskrit mine; for the original, see Deshpande 1989, 162):

> Deep inside my body I searched and searched for my soul.
> There was no soul there to be found but You, only You.

Compare this with Lalla's account of her own quest, cast as a lover's journey in search of an elusive Beloved, in poem 11:

> I, Lalla, wore myself down searching for Him
> and found a strength after my strength had died.
> I came to His threshold but found the door bolted.
> I locked that door with my eyes and looked at Him.

4. The Tantric Underground

> Up, woman! Go make your offering.
> Take wine, meat and a cake fit for the gods.
> If you know the password to the Supreme Place,
> you can reach wisdom by breaking the rules.
>
> (POEM 19)

Since explicit references to Tantric rites appear in a number of Lalla's *vākhs*, as in poem 19, we must attend to the probable circumstances of her association with the Tantric path. The figure of her predecessor, Abhinavagupta, thus forms an appropriate link between the previous section of this Introduction and the present one: he incarnated both the intellectual rigour of Kashmir Śaivism and the seemingly heterodox practice of the Tantras. To conventionally raised Hindus, it may appear inconceivable that an intellectual who wrote authoritative accounts of aesthetic experience and spiritual perfection could also write the *Tantrāloka* or 'The Radiance of the Tantras'. In the twenty-ninth chapter of this work, he elaborates on the rites of *Kulācāra*, which involve the cultivation of control over psychic processes and various forms of visualisation; these rites also include the controlled use of substances proscribed by the orthodoxy (such as wine, meat and fish) and taboo relationships (such as with women married to others, or far below the aspirant's caste status, or too intimately related to him). This is how, in Lalla's phrase, the aspirant may 'reach wisdom by breaking the rules'.

These rites were designed to incite the *sādhaka* or spiritual aspirant's consciousness into transcending the binaries governing acceptable social behaviour and the prevailing system of cultural assumptions. This was achieved by striking repeatedly at injunction and inhibition with transgression; by dramatising the dissolution of all differences between the sanctified and the unholy, the pure and the impure, the appropriate and the inappropriate, the permitted and the forbidden, under carefully regulated conditions presided over by an adept. Heinrich Zimmer's explanation of the logic of *Kulācāra* helps us situate Lalla's poems 19 and 20 in their correct context:

> Just as deadly poisons administered at the right time and in proper dosages can save a life, so too, *Kulācāra* prescribes things forbidden in everyday life as components of its rite that will reveal to the initiate the path to his becoming

divine [that is: recognising that he is, in fact, Shiva]. These ingredients are called, for brevity's sake, the 'five M's' (Ma-kāra-pancaka): alcohol (madya), meat (māmsa), fish (matsya), and illicit intercourse (maithuna); the fifth is the positioning of the hand and fingers (mudrā) ... It is not so much their basic ability to intoxicate and liberate a person that makes them into sacramental elements, but rather the fact that they have the power, ennobled by rite and enshrined in ceremony, to transport the initiate beyond the moral order of his everyday existence. (1984, 216–17)

*

The liberation of the sādhaka's consciousness from the regime of duality was paramount, not only to Tantra, but also to a variety of other spiritual projects that had announced themselves across India between the tenth and the fourteenth centuries CE. Among the exponents of these projects, we find the Tantrayāna Buddhists who wove Śaivite and Tantric ideas of redemption, together with Mahāyāna Buddhist ideas of soteriology, into a new fabric. We find, also, the Pāśupata renouncers who deliberately behaved in counter-social ways to invite the scorn and abuse necessary to break down the body-centred individual ego. From this period, also, date the investigations of the Siddha magician-poets who pursued the goal of rasāyana or alchemy, both at a material and a spiritual level. Their contemporaries, the Nātha ascetics, dedicated themselves to the quest for the nectar at the heart of experience, looking not only for salvation from the cycle of rebirth but also attempting to extend the dynamism and longevity of the physical organism beyond their natural span. These heterodox questors established a sacred geography of migration paths and staging points across the Indian subcontinent, so that, even today, their presence is memorialised, if not always recognised, in regions as diverse and seemingly far apart as Kashmir and Karnataka, Bengal and Maharashtra, Punjab and Madhya Pradesh, Baluchistan and Uttar Pradesh.

Distributed throughout the LD corpus lie themes that would instantly be acknowledged as central by all these practitioners: the analogy proposed between the interior reality of the yogini and the reality of the cosmos; the tension between breaking down the body-centred ego while refining the body as the vehicle of the soul; and the spiritual quest as an all-possessing and all-transforming pursuit, which places the seeker at a tangent to society, as an eccentric, a holy fool, an inspired lunatic.

In poem 80, for instance, Lalla offers the aspirant the following counsel, intended to contain the body's claims:

Wear just enough to keep the cold out,
eat just enough to keep hunger from your door.
Mind, dream yourself beyond Self and Other.
Remember, this body is just pickings for jungle crows.

But in poem 141, she proposes another and more Nātha-like way of relating to the body:

True mind, look inside this body,
this body they call the Self's own form.
Strip off greed and lust, polish this body,
this body as bright as the sun.

In poems 92 and 93, already quoted in this Introduction, Lalla courts the insults and curses of her detractors. Her talisman against these assaults is an indifference born of her conviction that she 'belongs to Shiva'. She treats them merely as ashes with which to clean the mirror of her consciousness (mirrors, in the historical Lalla's day, were made of metal and not glass). We may usefully compare Lalla's position in these poems with a laconic teaching of Lakuliśa or 'The Lord of the Mace', the founder of the Pāśupata cult: 'Ill-treated, he should wander.' His commentator, Kaundinya, offers the following gloss on this teaching, which is described as 'the seeking of dishonour':

> This ill treatment should be regarded as a coronation to a poor man . . . [The aspirant] should wander under false accusations on the principle that he who is dishonoured is on [the path to] acquiring merit . . . Hereby he becomes cut off from the respectable castes and conditions of men, and the power of passionless detachment is produced. (quoted in McEvilley 2002, 226)

At the same time, Lalla was keenly aware of the charlatanry of the lower kind of wandering renouncer: the renegade Siddha, Nātha or Yogi who, falling away from the spiritual quest yet retaining superficial abilities of telekinesis and bodily control, could dazzle the populace of householders with his bag of tricks. In poem 119, she frames a sardonic critique of such bazaar magicians:

> To dam a flood,
> to blow out a forest fire,
> to walk on air,
> to milk a wooden cow:
> any con artist could do it.

The apparent tension between the householder's way and the renouncer's path—and the delusion that the act of making a choice between them automatically marks the difference between ignorance and enlightenment—also exercised the ninth-century Siddha master Saraha, who meditated on the 'fair tree of the Void' at the confluence of Tantra and Mahāyāna Buddhism. As Saraha sang in his Dōhākośa or 'Treasury of Rhymed Couplets' (the translation from the Angika, a form of proto-Hindi, is D.L. Snellgrove's; Conze 1959, 179):

> Do not sit at home, do not go to the forest,
> But recognise mind wherever you are.
> When one abides in complete and perfect
> > enlightenment,
> Where is Samsara and where is Nirvana?
>
> O know this truth,
> That neither at home nor in the forest does enlightenment
> > dwell.
> Be free from prevarication
> In the self-nature of immaculate thought!

The intertextuality that relates Lalla's texts to those produced within her background traditions, which I have underscored in the context of her Kashmir Śaiva lineage, is dramatically visible and audible in the context of her Siddha affiliations as well. Five centuries after Saraha, Lalla employs the same imagery as he does, to confirm his diagnosis that illumination is not guaranteed to a renouncer or withheld from a householder; it comes to those who refine themselves to receive it. Lalla says:

Some run away from home, some escape the hermitage.
No orchard bears fruit for the barren mind.
Day and night, count the rosary of your breath,
and stay put wherever you are.

(POEM 122)

Hermit or householder: same difference.
If you've dissolved your desires in the river of time,
you will see that the Lord is everywhere and is perfect.
As you know, so shall you be.

(POEM 123)

*

The texts of the Pāśupata, Siddha and Nātha lineages were not
fossil fuel, but renewable resources: in Lalla's poetry, we find a
crucible in which they were fused at a new, intense and startling
level of expression. This would, therefore, be the appropriate
juncture at which to dwell on the genealogy of Lalla's *vākh* as a
literary form, and to accord it what I believe to be its rightful
place in that family of more than twenty poetic forms which are
grouped under the generic title of the *dōhā*. We may begin with
one of Grierson's speculations, made in an appendix to his 1920
edition. While investigating the subject of Kashmiri prosody,
he noted that, during the eighteenth and nineteenth centuries,
Kashmiri writers customarily used formal Persian metres such
as the *hazaj*, whether they were Muslims writing in Persian on
Islamic epic subjects or Pandits writing in Sanskrit on Hindu
philosophical or devotional themes. But the metrical system
used in Kashmiri songs, under which rubric Lalla's *vākhs* were

classified, was quite unique. Unlike the metrical system used in North India, which is based on syllabic quantity, the measure of the Kashmiri song depended on a sequence of stress-accents. In Lalla's poems, as Grierson notes, 'four stresses go to each *pada*, or line . . . [they] will not scan according to Indian rules, but nevertheless [their] lilt is strongly suggestive of the Indian *dōhā*'. Having arrived at this potentially historic insight, Grierson settles down to analyse the structure of the *dōhā*, usually developed as a rhymed couplet read as four half-lines. He breaks the *dōhā* down into the instants of voiced duration it takes up (with one instant corresponding to one short syllable, and a long syllable counting as two instants; the standard term for Grierson's 'instants' is *mātrās* or morae) and shows that the *dōhā* may be scanned as the following pattern of instants, or moraic count:

$$6 + 4 + 3 \mid 6 + 4 + 1$$
$$6 + 4 + 3 \mid 6 + 4 + 1$$

The same moraic count appears in many of Lalla's *vākhs*, with the four half-lines opened out into a quatrain:

$$6 + 4 + 3$$
$$6 + 4 + 1$$
$$6 + 4 + 3$$
$$6 + 4 + 1$$

Unfortunately, despite his pioneering work in the study of Indian linguistics and literature, Grierson remained committed to the top-down model of cultural transmission that was pervasive among intellectuals of his class, education, citizenship and epoch. Their liberal outlook and encyclopaedic interests were tempered by their membership of the Club of Imperial Certitude. Convinced that only an elite could produce serious culture, and that cultural materials always become degenerate and vulgarised when they descend from the elite to the masses, he concluded that Lalla's poems 'were originally intended to be based on some standard metre, but that in the mouths of the rustics stress became substituted for quantity' (1920, 144–48) Grierson chose to round off his sketch with the dismissive suggestion that Lalla's prosody was merely a demotic and irregular version of that practised by classical Prakrit poets such as the Sātavāhana ruler Hāla. Had he taken his metrical speculations—and his notion that the *vākh* scansion was of ultimately Central Asian origin—to their logical conclusion, he might have been able to situate Lalla's *vākhs* far more securely in a pan-Indian atlas of sacred poetry.

To demonstrate that this can be done, I will take recourse to Karine Schomer's fine paper, 'The Dōhā as a Vehicle of Sant Teachings'. While being concerned with the use of this family of poetic forms in the religious literature of the northern Indian Sant tradition, of the fourteenth to sixteenth centuries, especially in the poetry of Dādu and Kabīr, Schomer assembles an impressive genealogy for the *dōhā*. Crucially, for our purposes here, she amplifies the kind of prosodic analysis that Grierson essays briefly into a detailed examination of the structure of parallelism, opposition and surprise that gives the *dōhā* its special flavour, ensuring that it is 'not only brief and easy to remember, but also highly persuasive, carrying about it an aura of traditional wisdom and universal truth'. Signalling the Kashmiri *vākh* as an equivalent 'folk meter', Schomer observes that the *dōhā* came into being, historically, as 'a new kind of verse form closely associated with the rise of Apabhramśa . . . an extremely flexible meter based on *mātrā* or moraic count alone . . . its form [suggesting] oral composition and sung performance'. Noting, in a sophisticated recursion of Grierson's notion, that the meter may have been associated with the Ābhiras, a foreign people who entered India through the northwest during the early first millennium and who were known to have influenced the development of Apabhramśa, Schomer writes that the *dōhā*

> became the dominant meter of Apabhramśa, just as the *gāthā* was the dominant meter of Prakrit and the *śloka* of Sanskrit . . . Indeed, the *dōhā* is prominent in all of the different kinds of Apabhramśa literature that have come down to us: grammars and works on metrics, Jain didactic anthologies and religious narratives, secular love narratives, *the utterances of the Buddhist Siddhas, doctrinal works of the Kashmir Śaivas, the vernacular literature of the Nātha Yogis* and, finally, poetry in praise of kings, including the early *rāso* literature of Rajasthan. (emphasis mine)

In course of time, Schomer writes, 'the *dōhā* became an omni-purpose meter' and assumed two major functions, those of 'the compressed aphoristic statement, i.e. proverbial utterance or folk saying' and the 'lyrical evocation of intense feeling' that may have 'evolved out of women's folksongs' (1987, 63–66).

This, in my view, is the real linguistic and literary continuum within which Lalla's *vākhs*—emerging as they originally did at the threshold between Apabhramśa and modern Kashmiri, relaying the energies of the one into the other—must be historically situated. Lalla was an exceptional poet, but I would like to show that she was not, in historical terms, the inexplicable singularity, the puzzling exception, the isolated oddity that she is often made out to be.

*

I believe that this living archive of philosophical and literary resources, communicated by the Śaivas, Siddhas and Nāthas, was urgently active in the formation and orientation of the historical Lalla's world-view and poetry. The confluence of these forces suggests, to me, that a substantial, vigorous and heterodox counterculture existed in Kashmir between the tenth and the fourteenth centuries. Accordingly, I would argue that the historical Lalla clearly drew on and, to some extent, participated in this counterculture, which I will name the 'Tantric underground'. Aligned with its counterparts elsewhere in the Indian subcontinent, it would have served as a fertile ground for new spiritual developments. From the available information about the various groups and lineages whose texts, narratives and practices circulated within it, as well as hints that we find in ritual manuals, I would speculate that the Tantric underground embodied a trans-caste movement. Indeed, this circumstance may have done much to reduce and mitigate, in late mediaeval and early modern Kashmir, the explosive caste tensions that were prevalent elsewhere in the subcontinent during that period. The diffusion of Islam has traditionally been given the credit for this unusual disappearance of intra-caste solidarity and inter-caste antagonism in Kashmir (the old identities now survive among Kashmiri Muslims only as surnames such as Bhat, Mattoo and

Katju, and kram or clan names such as Dar, Lone and Tantri, with no corresponding system of caste identification or endogamous exclusivity). But the seeds of social change may well have been sown a few centuries before the advent of the Sufis in the Valley. The conventional schema of the battle for the hearts and minds of Kashmiris in the late mediaeval period has been represented as a contest between Brahminical Hinduism and Sufi Islam; this third and potent alternative, the Tantric underground, has been lying concealed, in the form of isolated traces scattered across various disciplines of study, without a context to unify them and disclose their significance.

Significantly, in *Kulācāra*, the catalytic figures who induce the *sādhaka* to liberate his consciousness belong to the subaltern castes. The paramount *chakra* sacrifice involves the presence and activities of 'nine wives': women of ritually impure status who are about to engage in adulterous intercourse. In detailing this secret ritual, Abhinavagupta describes these women as goddesses and observes that they are to be treated as such (while they no doubt reverted to their regular status by day, these transitions of status cannot have been entirely without effect on their self-consciousness and sense of agency). The most significant of these women is the *chakrinī* (Kashmiri: krōjü), the potter's wife, who occupies the centre of the circle and acts as the yogi's sexual partner (Dupuche 2003, 116–23; see, also, the note to poem 33).

The meticulously choreographed *yonipujā*, or ritual with a sexual partner, also involves a 'forbidden' woman. The adept gives her a narcotic drink and wine, and ritually anoints her with vermilion and sandalpaste; he then conducts what is described as 'ritual coition' with her, before retreating to ceremonially worship her yoni (Dupuche 2003, 124–35). It is clear that these esoteric rites ran the risk of lapsing into crassly self-indulgent and exploitative excess. It is also clear that they remain, from the textual evidence, dedicated to the psycho-spiritual transcendence of a male rather than a female practitioner, with little concern for the efficacy or otherwise of the ritual for the women involved (apart from what we may speculate about the sense of agency that their liminal status may have conferred on them).

Richard Lannoy contextualises the Tantric path within the model of what he terms the 'social Antipodes', the axial relationship of mutual opposition and attraction that conjoins the higher castes, and their orthodox world view, with the lower castes and tribal society, and their multiple heterodoxies.

There are many examples of the interplay between the repressive and libidinous elements in Hindu society. For instance, on the one hand the extremely strict rules imposed on the upper caste stratum reveal a high degree of psychological repression which accompanies the advance of civilisation, while on the other hand the most characteristic feature of Indian culture is the persistent vitality, not to say obtrusiveness, of its folk cultures . . . the most striking example is undoubtedly the relation between Tantric Hinduism (a revalorisation of primitive magic and ritualised orgiasticism) and the more ascetic and puritanical Brahminical orthodoxy . . . The personal underground of the subconscious high-caste mind feeds [its] consciousness from below. Every well-documented case of a great creative Indian personality abounds in

evidence of such contacts with the non-rational culture
of excluded peoples and classes. (1971, 170–71)

By contrast with this perspicacious analysis, the horror of some
twentieth-century Kashmiri historians at Tantra is undoubtedly
conditioned by the internalised perspective of the Victorian
missionary appalled by heathen proceedings. Presumably
P.N.K. Bamzai had performances like the *chakra* sacrifice in mind
when he wrote of late mediaeval Hinduism in Kashmir, mixing
categories and inverting causalities somewhat: 'Saktism, born
of the love for Durga worship, had degenerated into grotesque
forms of rites and ceremonies' (1994, 2:550).

In Lalla's case, the evidence suggests that she worked her way
across the Tantric path, using it as a bridge rather than a platform.
Exquisitely reminding us that the Tantras have a conceptual as
well as a physical basis, and that the transgressions they demand
are as spiritual in nature as they are social, Lalla translates the
details and ingredients of the expressly Tantric ceremony of poem
19 into an allegory and a cautionary tale in poem 20:

Fatten the five elements like they were rams meant for
                                                    the sacrifice.
Feed them the grain of mind-light, and cakes fit for
                                                    the gods.
Then kill them. But don't rush.
You need the password to the Supreme Place
to reach wisdom by breaking the rules.

*

With some reason, therefore, Tantric practice is popularly identified with the ritual use of sexuality, the symbolism of decay and death, and other features that seem to stand at the profane end of the spectrum of human activities, very remote from the sacred. Unfortunately inspired by this, some enthusiasts, usually of European, American or expatriate Indian location, have sensationalised Tantra as an exotic way of life that can somehow be mapped onto a bohemian lifestyle. Their approach overlooks the fact that the static binary opposition has no place in Hindu thought, which sees all opposites as being engaged in constant and dynamic interplay. Thus, the sacred and the profane, like the ascetic and the erotic or the festive and the melancholy, interpenetrate and transform one another as well as the consciousness that dwells upon their interplay.

On the other hand, many Hindus who believe themselves to be orthodox regard the Tantras with profound suspicion, and unimaginable perversions have been attributed to this more occluded aspect of Hindu religious life. Some commentators have demanded the excision of the Tantras from a Hinduism that must be read back to an imagined Vedic purity or 'reformed', that is to say, purified of its ambiguities and bowdlerised to eliminate its stimulating perplexities. This kind of reform—as against the struggle to rid Hinduism of the persisting asymmetries of caste and patriarchal sanction—is merely an attempt to render Hindu religious practice palatable to a modern bourgeoisie for whom religion is an insurance policy, bought to protect it from the moral consequences of its own deceits, compromises and hypocrisies.

Such a refusal to cope with the differential perspectives within the Hindu rubric stems also from the widespread misconception that all Hinduism is reducible to Vedānta. This misconception was originally perpetuated by colonial scholarship, since it conveniently justified the stereotype of the passive and otherworldly 'Hindoo' who saw the world as illusion, had no desire to govern himself, and whose resources could therefore be siphoned away while he dreamt of fusing self with Overself.[6] It has long since been internalised by Hindus themselves, in an act of auto-Orientalism that has had debilitating consequences for the theory as well as the practice of Hinduism.

To condemn the Tantric path as an exploration of perversity is to forget that it has provided a crucial rite of passage to numerous spiritual questors through the centuries, and even to so incomparable a modern master as Sri Ramakrishna Paramahamsa. The transition that the priest of Kāli at Dakshineshwar made, from a spontaneous and unstructured God-intoxication to the flowering of spiritual awareness, was catalysed by his demanding two-year Tantric discipleship with the woman guru, Bhairavi Brahmani, over 1861–63. The contemporary teacher and commentator, Swami Niranjanananda Saraswati of the Bihar School of Yoga, interprets the Tantras as essaying a complex resolution of a fundamental conflict: between the raw physical energies and instinctual drives on the one hand, and the field of expanding intelligence and consciousness on the other. Instead of repressing the sexual appetites, the craving for security, the force of irrationality and the various emotional syndromes generated by repression, Tantric techniques draw these out, empty them of negativity, and harmonise them into a more integrated, fulfilling and creative pattern of being (1995, 1:95–102)

*

5. Lalla's Utterance and Her Community of Interlocutors

What the books taught me, I've practised.
What they didn't teach me, I've taught myself.
I've gone into the forest and wrestled with the lion.
I didn't get this far by teaching one thing and
        doing another.

(POEM 111)

In the twenty years that I have spent studying and translating Lalla's *vākhs*, I have repeatedly marvelled at how powerfully verb-driven they are. Rich as they are in visual image, cunning in their music and scintillating in the metaphorical leaps they make, these poems turn most crucially on their action words. And there is nothing reticent, passive or gentle about these: *tsāṭun-wāṭun*, to cut, hack or rip, and bind; *rāṭun*, to seize, grapple or wrestle; *nērē*, *drāyun*, to go forth, roam or wander; *gwārun*, to hunt or search energetically; *prawād kôrun*, to shout or proclaim. In poem 13, Lalla hugs the teacher whom she finds waiting for her at home; in poems 49 and 50, she roasts her heart, while in 50, she pestles it. In poem 51, she pictures her body as a burning coal; in 47, she mixes with the Divine and drowns herself; in 68, again, she throws herself into the lake of nectar.

Lalla's signature line, too, articulates this spirited engagement of a bodied individual with the world: 'Lal bŏh' or a syntactical variation on it, meaning 'I, Lalla'. It appears in sixteen of the 146 poems translated here (although, depending on my reading of the demands of the *vākh* as shaped newly in the target language, I have not rendered it as such in every case). Usually, this signature line acts as a prelude to action, the assertion of a particular self through performance. It does not signal a sardonic or meditative conclusion appended to a train of thought, and in this, is markedly different in its operation from the signature lines employed by some of the prominent male saint-poets who emerged between the fifteenth and seventeenth centuries, including Kabīr (whose signature line is 'kahat Kabīrā' or 'says Kabīr') and Tukārām (whose signature line, likewise, is 'Tukā mhaṇé' or 'says Tukā').

The Lalla whose presence animates these 146 vākhs, with her performative sense of self and her physicality of phrase, is no recluse or pining bride of God. The forms of address that she uses while engaging with priests, scholars, teachers, and even the Divine can be very direct and informal, shorn of decorum. In poems 58, 59 and 114, priests and scholars get short shrift as she challenges their methods and convictions: 'hōṭa baṭā', 'Hey priest-man!' And yet she can speak tenderly to the guru or the Divine, calling him 'Māli', 'Father', or 'Siddhō', 'Master', or 'Nātha', 'Dear Lord'. More formally yet still lovingly, she can praise the Divine as 'Sura-guru-nātha', 'the Teacher who is First among the Gods'. But even with the Divine, Lalla can sometimes be disconcertingly familiar: in poem 24, she calls Shiva 'Shyāma-galā', 'Blue-throated One'. She refers to the Divine as Shiva in eighteen of the 146 poems in this edition, also using Shiva's other names, such as Hara, Shambhu and Shankara (poems 3, 24, 49, 60, 61, 64, 78, 98–104, 134–36; I have not consistently replicated Shiva's allonyms wherever they occur). Shiva and Shakti appear together in two poems (68 and 115). Other Hindu divinities also appear in Lalla's hymns and allegories. Vishnu, in his aspects as Kĕshĕv (the Kashmiri for Keshava) and Nārān (the Kashmiri for Nārāyana) graces poems 3, 7, 16 and 78. Brahma, whom Lalla calls Kamal-aza-nāth (the Kashmiri for Kamalajanātha, the 'lotus-born Lord'), is mentioned in 3 and 78; as is the Mother Goddess in poem 65; and the Buddha, under the designation Zin, which I explain in the Notes, in poem 3.

As noted already, the guru plays an important role in Lalla's account of the spiritual journey, and is referred to in various guises in nineteen of the present poems: as master or guide, hermit or sage, wise man or naked ascetic. In some of the vākhs, Lalla puts questions about Yogic practice to her teacher, and receives clarifications. In other vākhs, she herself is the guru, variously composing a teaching poem to inspire an aspirant, a robust re-affirmation of purpose for an initiate, a contemplative residuum of experience to be shared with a fellow adept, or a piece of tough talk aimed by a stern instructor at a backslider along the path. As she says in poem 111, placed at the head of this section, she was both a student and an autodidact, learning from her masters and their books but also enrolling herself in the university of experience. Thus Lalla's vākhs can often, though not invariably, assume the form of the wŏpadĕsh—cognate with the Sanskrit upadeśa—or lesson. This could be a note of advice, rebuke or provocation; or an ironic wake-up call for those who miss the subtle point of a master's direction; or a message that, far from reassuring its recipients, disturbs them out of their complacency.

Indeed, the way in which Lalla's poems mediate the conceptual space between the vākh and the wŏpadĕsh should encourage us to formulate a theory of utterance that links the two theatres of the mystic-poet's life: the inner world of solitary contemplation, prayer and visionary experience, and the outer world of the community, structured by social and political relationships. As inspired utterance, the *vākh* emerges from the first theatre: it attests to the transformation experience of an individual striving for an expansion of consciousness beyond language, and a dissolution of the private self in the awareness of cosmic totality. As teaching, the *wŏpadēsh* manifests itself in the second theatre, and is intended to communicate the energy of spiritual transformation to its auditors. It uses language to signal the contours of what is beyond language; but it also prompts its auditors to liberate themselves from the bonds of delusion, ignorance and dependence on sterile or exploitative systems of belief.

In this context, Lalla's preferred informality of address could be seen as a strategy of democratisation. We could speculate that the historical Lalla used colloquial and demotic forms to share the *wŏpadēsh* with an expanding community of interlocutors who took their cue from her and became the earliest members of the contributory lineage. Consider the various milieux in which Lalla's poetry came to be transmitted. While Lalla is recorded as having won the praise of Sufis like Baba Daud Mishkati and Baba Nasibuddin Ghazi (Khan 2002, 70–71), her poems were eventually also memorised by reciters associated with Śaivite teaching circles as part of their daily prayers and spiritual study (Kaul 1973, reprinted in Toshkhani 2002, 122), and sung by itinerant village bards (Kak 2007, 3). That there was a certain fluidity among these assemblies is evident from the symptomatic example of the overlap between the Darwēsh–Śastri–Grierson line of transmission and the Azizullah Khan poems. Gradually, as the *wŏpadēsh* circulated among these intersecting assemblies—priests and peasants, aspirants and adepts, Hindus and Muslims—it began to multiply across a range of registers, including the proclamation, the soliloquy, the lament, the dire prediction, the hymn and the love song for the Divine. Through the flow of these vākhs, we see how the author of the utterance and her successors produced themselves as rhetorical subjectivities, political actors. My purpose in insisting on the importance of the LD corpus is not to take away from the historical Lalla's agency, but to suggest how the contributory lineage, acting in her name, distributed her agency—and with it, the privilege of articulation—among those who had no access to political influence, no stake in cultural hegemony. In retrieving the deep sources of the sacred from standard-issue religiosity and celebrating the individual questor's power to determine her own destiny, the historical Lalla and the contributors to the LD corpus staked out a mobile, self-renewing, uncontainable space of resistance to authority. As the speaker in poem 128 declares:

Master, leave these palm leaves and birch barks
to parrots who recite the name of God in a cage.
Good luck, I say, to those who think they've read
the scriptures.
The greatest scripture is the one that's playing in
my head.

*

There is no trace, in the vākhs, of Lalla's pre-questor biography as it is enshrined in the hagiographies: no complaints about the suspicious husband, the cruel mother-in-law, the stone in the plate, indeed, no reference at all to her domestic sufferings, unless a hint of these appears in poem 142:

> Don't think I did all this to get famous.
> I never cared for the good things of life.
> I always ate sensibly. I knew hunger well,
> and sorrow, and God.

What the *vākhs* record, instead, is the biography of an individual actively seeking enlightenment, defying the orthodoxy, subjecting the fossil habits of religion to critique, and learning to cope in various ways with the irruption of the Divine into her life. And it is a vigorous outdoor life that Lalla leads, connected to the materiality of the everyday, which is sensuously apprehended. Her poetry moves seamlessly between the metaphysical realm of the cultivated breath, the opened lotus of consciousness and vatic ecstasy on the one hand, and the domain of objects, tools, social relationships and human emotions on the other. This is why I am surprised by the suggestions, made by several scholars, that Lalla's poems are replete with references to women's work or domestic details. For instance, Neerja Mattoo, having observed that Lalla 'conversed and discussed with the most learned scholars—all men—of her time on an equal footing', goes on to advance the claim that 'there is no elitist, Brahminical choice of word, phrase or metaphor—these are drawn from a woman's world of domesticity, even though she walked out of marriage and home. Her poetry is a woman's work and in the process she gives a voice to women' (in Toshkhani 2002, 69). As we know, Lalla's poetry demonstrates an opulence of technical terms, even if its philosophy is imparted through stunningly visceral symbolism. And, with all due respect to feminist commentators, the domestic realm of women is conspicuously absent in these *vākhs*. There is barely a glimpse of the domestic interior in these 146 poems: Lalla was a wanderer across the landscapes of river, lake and snow, and no stranger to boat, anchor and tow-rope.

In actuality—and this may reflect the likelihood that the LD corpus has had a preponderance of male contributors—the choice of recurrent imagery in the *vākhs* offers testimony to a criss-crossing of gender lines. Lalla's poems draw considerably on artisanal and mercantile life: masonry and the building trades are prominent in poems 28 and 71; the shepherd plays a role in poem 10, the carpenter in 12, the blacksmith in 18, the cook in 31, and the cleaner, carder, spinner and weaver in 38, and the washerman and tailor in 39. The tools and weapons of male labour are harnessed to symbolic purpose: the bellows in poems 18 and 52, the sabre in 96, the bow and arrow in 12 and 84, the whip in 56, and the harpoon in 86; poems 40 and 56 hinge on the act of flaying or cutting and measuring a hide.

The horse, a proud spirit barely tamed by the rider's apparatus of saddle, bridle, rein and stirrup, dominates poems 76–79, 108 and 137. The marketplace is the site where allegories are staged in poems 12 and 26; the garland-maker and his wife occupy a crucial metaphorical position in 66 and 67. Nautical equipment—the ferry, the pier, towing, the net and the anchor—occurs in poems 4, 5, 6, 7, 105, 125. The garden, variously boasting jasmine, saffron and narcissus, forms the occasion for several poems, including 65, 68, 69 and 83, to unfold. The road, the river, the lake, the embankment and the bridge provide the setting for many of Lalla's meditations. The traversal of the landscape is often a traversal of the transcendent states that she names the Field of Emptiness or the Field of Light, experiencing these during what are clearly shamanic transports of the spirit beyond its quotidian confines. By contrast, the world of female labour conducted in domestic interiors appears only in five poems: through the image of the grain mill in 21, 22, 90 and 99, and of the hearth in 33.

Lalla's poetry demonstrates close acquaintance with the raw side of life. In poem 69, Death chases the soul like a tax-collector, exacting his dues. The addressee in poem 83 is told that he cannot put up a proxy to be executed in his place; it is his own 'neck on the block'. In poem 144, Yama, the Lord of Death, sends his warders to drag 'delusion's captive' away, bleeding: the reference is to a brutal method of punishment, *chōra-dārĕ karun*, in which the prisoner is dragged along stony ground until he bleeds almost to death. In its figurative, even figural language, the LD corpus has encoded the idioms of social, political and juridical violence prevalent in Kashmir between the thirteenth and the nineteenth centuries.

*

6. Translation: Methods and Reasons

> Wear the robe of wisdom,
> brand Lalla's words on your heart,
> lose yourself in the soul's light,
> you too shall be free.

(POEM 146)

I, *Lalla* is a new translation of Lalla's poetry for twenty-first-century readers. In preparing it, I have gone back to the original, word by word, line by line, clause by clause. My method has been geared, not to achieving a rigidly lexical and metrical counterpart of the source language, but to trawl for the play of resonance and intertextuality around and through the words. This is essential, in order to convey Lalla's compressions, condensations, allusions, dual meanings and coded signals. She is a demanding poet, by turns illuminating and occluded, candid and dissembling, a woman who does not throw her words away. My attempt has been to bring across into English the jagged, epiphanic power of Lalla's poetry; to restore the colloquial pulse of her voice; and to retrieve the ideas, images and tonalities of the LD corpus from the metaphysical glosses that have often usurped their place in the minds of readers.

In the process, this translation is intended to strip away a century of ornate, Victorian-inflected renderings and paraphrases, and to disclose the grain and tenor of Lalla's voice, the orality, vocality and spokenness of her poems. Most existing translations of the *vākhs* are hobbled by three major problems. First, a number of them are reworkings of Grierson and Barnett's 1920 versions, built on the basis of phrasal variants on that English text rather than on fresh efforts to address the Kashmiri original. Secondly, most of them suffer from the desire to sound 'poetical', and deliver themselves in the ponderous idiom—part Edwin Arnold, part Leigh Hunt, with a dash of Tennyson—that was once thought appropriate to the rendering of 'Oriental' religious literature into English. Such poeticality is the enemy of poetry, and is especially tragic when employed by writers whose prose is perfectly contemporary. And thirdly, a number of these translations rush past the word to embrace the spirit, or what the translator believes to be the spirit, substituting Lalla's palpable immediacy with philosophical abstraction. Elliptical and often laconic as they are, the vākhs cannot be translated *as* commentary.

I have chosen to present the 146 vākhs that I have translated here in a sequence that suggests the journey of an evolving religious imagination, from the phase of self-doubt to those, successively, of visionary experience, the discovery of wisdom, and the sharing of that wisdom through teaching. This sequence is arranged in a fluid and associative order, however, rather than according to a strictly graduated logic: I have not divided it into sections, because I would like every vākh in this collection to relate to every other, without forcing linkages among them.

*

I began this translation of Lal Děd's poems in February 1991, a month short of twenty-two; I am nearly forty-two as I come to the end of the process. For two decades, my copies of the *Lal vākh*, of Grierson and Barnett's 1920 edition, Jayalal Kaul's 1973 study and Shiban Krishna Raina's Hindi paraphrases have accompanied me everywhere. I shared the earliest drafts of this translation, as work-in-progress, with colleagues at Daniel Weissbort's translation workshop when I was a Fellow of the International Writing Program at the University of Iowa in 1995. I have listened to the cadence of the vākhs in Province town, Istanbul, Vienna, Tokyo, Gholvad, Cambridge, New Delhi, Munich, New York, Berlin, Pune, Brisbane, Zürich, Heidelberg, Oslo and Utrecht, and in none of these locales did Lal Děd seem a stranger. At home in Bombay, a cabinet of Lalla-related books, photocopies, notes and drafts has served me as a geniza.

I began to translate Lalla because she provided a connection to an ancestral past, to a homeland and a language that I had lost, as the descendant of Kashmiri Saraswat Brahmins who migrated to southwestern India in several waves of diaspora between the tenth and fourteenth centuries. Translating Lalla allowed me to learn the language of my ancestors; or rather, the language I might have spoken as a matter of course, had my ancestors not emigrated from the Valley. And beyond this archaeology into my own ethnic past lay the beauty and energy of the verses: in these twenty years, I have lived with the intricacies of Lalla's language, its familiar yet cryptic phonetics, the surprises hidden in its web of references. When I began working on this translation, I was attempting to reconcile the political and cultural perspectives of the anarchist and Marxian traditions with everything that I had assimilated in the course of a somewhat unusual upbringing whose varied elements included Kashmir Śaivite philosophy, Vaiṣṇava devotionalism, Buddhist reading, Sufi stories, a family connection with Theosophy and the teachings of J. Krishnamurti, an early childhood spent in Catholic South Goa and a colonial-style Presbyterian schooling in Bombay.

As I continued to study and translate Lalla through the 1990s and 2000s—a period overshadowed by the forces of neo-conservative organised religion and militantly politicised religiosity—I was able, gradually, to disentangle my antagonism towards these forces from the more enduring quest for the sacred, with which they have nothing in common. The project of translating Lalla has altered my perceptions of religious belief, of the nature of faith and of the questor's journey. My long apprenticeship to Lalla has also honed my receptivity to the challenges of engaging with different realms of experience, finding an appropriate voice for them: here, the experience of a religious seeker, a social rebel, a woman. The translator is always humbled, broken and re-made in the act of translation.

*

The duration of my apprenticeship to Lalla has been mapped across the rise of an aggressive Hindu majoritarianism that threatened the core values of the Indian Republic; and equally, the consolidation of a global Islamism, flying under the banner of Salafism or Jihad, that is intolerant of difference. These two movements mirror one another in their desire to replace an actual diversity of cultural and philosophical expressions with an imposed singularity of belief, and are most dangerous to Hinduism and Islam, the religions whose interests they claim respectively to represent. My political purpose in undertaking this translation is to make a small intervention in the debate provoked by the contention of these rival forms of politicised religiosity in India: Hindutva and Islamism, twins in annihilatory intolerance, ranged against the pluralist and multi-perspectival tradition of the Indian subcontinent as well as against the liberal and Constitutional order of the modern Indian nation-state. In an epoch dominated by majoritarianism, sectarian intolerance and the deployment of faith as a political instrument, Lalla asserts the duty of critical intelligence, to be exercised alongside the right to belief.

This translation is offered in the spirit of sharing, with those who have no access to it, an uncommon resource of regeneration for the embattled spirit. And yet, as I write these words, which suggest that those within Kashmir have direct access to Lalla, I find myself admitting that she is an absence in the Kashmir of today. Even as we look on, the region's confluential and multi-religious culture, the culture of Lal Dĕd and Nund Rishi, is being swept away. A generation of Muslim children have grown up in Kashmir, who have never known Hindus. Their counterparts, a generation of children born to the Kashmiri Pandits who escaped terrorism in the early 1990s, have grown up in refugee camps in Jammu and elsewhere in northern India. They have no first-hand acquaintance with Kashmir or Kashmiri Muslims. Kashmir's special form of Islam is in retreat before a monolithic pan-Islamic approach, which is being promoted in the name of purity—of doctrine and practice. On the other hand, Kashmiri Hinduism has been destroyed. Pandit shrines are now run by Hindu priests from the plains, employed by the armed forces; to these outsiders, many elements of Pandit ritual practice would seem either strange or positively anathema (see the notes to poems 58 and 59).

On a visit to Kashmir some years ago, during a lull in what many Kashmiris euphemistically call the 'turmoil', we found the streets bristling with sand-bagged gun emplacements. Military units were on the move everywhere; and while a traders' strike was in force, business was being conducted elegantly from the back doors of stores. Wherever we went, once people had passed beyond the exchange of bland civilities and established a bond of trust, we were asked: 'Why does no one tell the world our story? Why have you forgotten us?' As we drove through the mountains, to Sheikh Balkhi's shrine in Pakhar Pora, surrounded by pine and cypress, and to the ruined sun temple of Mārtanda, built by Lalitāditya, I found tears in my eyes. The earth was alive with sturdy walnuts, tall pines, the poplars and flowering apricots of spring; but wherever there were settlements, we found a spiky creeper. It grew along the walls that surround public buildings and private homes; it curled around schools, mosques, abandoned temples, half-asleep hotels. Concertina wire is the most widespread form of vegetation in Kashmir today. It grows everywhere, even in the mind.

Is Kashmir isolated in this predicament? Or does it, instead, epitomise the epic turbulence that afflicts South Asia? Everywhere in the subcontinent, we find regions deeply tormented by ideological and religious schisms, suffering the legacy of terror as well as the insensitivity and repression of a State that cannot fathom the true feelings of its people. Everywhere, too, we find individuals who are uncertain of whether their journey through these troubled landscapes will be a pilgrimage towards illumination or an excursion into nightmare. In the depths of this crisis, I would like to believe that Lalla's voice can still exert a redemptive power over those who hear her. As she says in poem 90:

Resilience: to stand in the path of lightning.
Resilience: to walk when darkness falls at noon.
Resilience: to grind yourself fine in the turning mill.
Resilience will come to you.

Bombay, December 2009 – Utrecht, September 2010

Notes

1. As Benedict Anderson writes, directing his observations to the European situation, in *Imagined Communities* (1991, 44–45):

Print-capitalism gave a new fixity to language, which in the long run helped to build that image of antiquity so central to the subjective idea of the nation. As Febvre and Martin remind us, the printed book kept a permanent form, capable of virtually infinite reproduction, temporally and spatially. It was no longer subject to the individualising and 'unconsciously modernising' habits of monastic scribes. Thus, while twelfth-century French differed markedly from that written by Villon in the fifteenth, the rate of change slowed decisively in the sixteenth. 'By the seventeenth century, languages in Europe had generally assumed their modern forms.' To put it another way, for three centuries now these stabilised print-languages have been gathering a darkening varnish; the words of our seventeenth-century forebears are accessible to us in a way that to Villon his twelfth-century ancestors were not.

Anderson characterises this process as arising largely unselfconsciously from the interplay among capitalism, technology and linguistic diversity. He notes, however, that once such fixity or stability was attained, it could be placed at the disposal of ideological agents motivated by a politics of nationalist (or subnationalist) identity as an instrument of mobilisation and consolidation.

2. I am thinking, especially, of the well-known and often retold miracle story about Lalla's encounter with the Sufi saint and missionary, Sayyid Ali Hamadani or Shah-i Hamadan. In this account, Lalla is cast as a 'mendicant devotee [who wandered] about the country singing and dancing in a half-nude condition', rejecting all notions of bodily shame. Once, on seeing the Sufi saint approach, she cried out, 'I have seen a man,' and, running into a bakery to conceal herself, leaped into the oven. By divine grace, she emerged from the flames dressed

in the effulgent robes of paradise, and presented herself before Shah-i Hamadan (Grierson and Barnett 1920, 2–3). The ideologically tuned implication that there were no real men in a still largely Hindu–Buddhist Kashmir is obvious, as is the advantage to be gained by presenting a leading Śaiva yogini in a state of submission before the most venerated Sufi in the Valley. The patriarchalist overtones of this story appear to have escaped those commentators who cite it as evidence of the influence of Sufism on Lalla's spirituality, or of the dialogue between Islam and Hinduism in Kashmir.

3. In this context, see the 1958 essay by Bernard S. Cohn and McKim Marriott, 'Networks and Centres in the Integration of Indian Civilisation'. In the course of their research, the authors identified several chains of religious, political and commercial specialists who hold the socially and culturally diverse networks of Indian society together. Among these are

> expert managers of cultural media [who mediate] between
> a more refined level of learning and the demands of the less
> learned, local market for their services. Specialists of any type
> in such multilevel hierarchies must look both down and up;
> because they constantly turn back and forth, Redfield had called
> them 'hinge' groups. (Cohn 1988, 83)

4. In his 1934–35 essay, 'Discourse in the Novel', Bakhtin distinguishes between norm and heteroglossia. While 'norm' refers to the centralising, unitary, ideological and centripetal legislations that aim to shape a language, 'heteroglossia' embodies the idiosyncratic, decentralising, unpredictable and centrifugal usage of varied groups, which actually constitutes the textures of that language and ensures its dynamic vitality and relevance. Bakhtin writes (1991, 272):

Every concrete utterance of a speaking subject serves as a point where centrifugal as well as centripetal forces are brought to bear. The processes of centralisation and decentralisation, of unification and disunification, intersect in the utterance; the utterance not only answers the requirements of its own language as an individualised embodiment of a speech act, but it answers the requirements of heteroglossia as well; it is in fact an active participant in such speech diversity. And this active participation of every utterance in living heteroglossia determines the linguistic profile and style of the utterance to no less a degree than its inclusion in any normative-centralising system of a unitary language ... Such is the fleeting language of a day, of an epoch, a social group, a genre, a school and so forth ... The authentic environment of an utterance, the environment in which it lives and takes shape, is dialogised heteroglossia, anonymous and social as language, but simultaneously concrete, filled with specific content and accented as an individual utterance.

5. The central doctrine of the Yogācāra or Vijñānavāda school of Mahāyāna Buddhism is *citta-mātra*, 'mind-only', which has often been misinterpreted to imply a solipsist or an extreme mentalist standpoint. As the Buddhist historian Andrew Skilton clarifies (1994, 123), *citta-mātra* does not mean that

everything is made of mind (as though the mind were some kind of universal matter), but that the totality of our experience is dependent upon our mind. The proposition is that we can only know or experience things with our mind. Even sense experience is cognised by the mind, therefore the things that we know, every element of our cognition, is essentially part of a mental process. Nothing cognised can be radically or fundamentally different from that mind.

This point is taken up and discussed more fully in the note to poem 86.

6. The early Orientalist and colonial jurist, Sir William Jones (1746–94), for instance, interpreted, as the 'fundamental tenet' of Vedanta, the belief that matter 'has no essence independent of mental perception, that existence and perceptibility are convertible terms, that external appearances and sensations are illusory, and would vanish into nothing, if the divine energy, which alone sustains them, were suspended but for a moment' (Pachori 1993, 194).

The Poems

1

One shrine to the next, the hermit can't stop for breath.
Soul, get this! You should have looked in the mirror.
Going on a pilgrimage is like falling in love
with the greenness of faraway grass.

2

I burnt up the landscape with footprints, looked for
                                    Him everywhere.
Then it hit me: What am I thinking, He's everywhere!
Lalla distilled this truth from a hundred pieces of talk.
Now hear this, people, and go mad!

3

Shiva or Keshava or the Enlightened One or the Lotus-born,
whatever He calls Himself,
I just wish He'd cure this poor woman of life,
be He He or He or He or He.

4

I'm towing my boat across the ocean with a thread.
Will He hear me and help me across?
Or am I seeping away like water from a half-baked cup?
Wander, my poor soul, you're not going home anytime soon.

5

Gently, gently I weep for you, my soul.
You've lost your heart to Mr Illusion.
You've forgotten who you are. And this iron anchor,
not even its shadow will remain behind when the time comes.

6

(This *vākh* has two alternative readings)

The road I came by wasn't the road I took to go.
As I stood on the embankment, breached and bridged,
                                        the day faded.
I looked in my purse and couldn't find the smallest coin
to give the ferryman.

or

The road I came by wasn't the road I took to go.
As I stood on my mind's embankment, the day faded.
I looked in my purse and couldn't find Shiva's name
to give the ferryman.

7

Brother, what's the point of twisting a rope of sand?
You couldn't tow a boat with that line.
The course that Nārāyana has charted for you,
no one can turn that around.

8

They kept coming, they kept coming, now they've got to go.
They've got to keep moving, day or night,
and where they came from, there they've got to go.
From nothing to nothing to nothing and why?

9

From what direction did I come, and by what road?
In what direction am I going, how shall I find the road?
I hope they'll send me a map before it's too late
or it's all over for me, my breath all gone to waste.

10

I'm carrying this sack of candy, its knot gone slack on
                                        my shoulder.
I took a wrong turn and wasted my day, what's to be done?
I'm lost, my teacher's warning blisters me like a whiplash.
This flock has no shepherd, what's to be done?

11

I, Lalla, wore myself down searching for Him
and found a strength after my strength had died.
I came to His threshold but found the door bolted.
I locked that door with my eyes and looked at Him.

12

My willow bow was bent to shoot, but my arrow was only grass.
A klutz of a carpenter botched the palace job I got him.
In the crowded marketplace, my shop stands unlocked.
Holy water hasn't touched my skin. I've lost the plot.

13

Love-mad, I, Lalla, started out,
spent days and nights on the trail.
Circling back, I found the teacher in my own house.
What brilliant luck, I said, and hugged him.

14

I wore myself out, looking for myself.
No one could have worked harder to break the code.
I lost myself in myself and found a wine cellar. Nectar, I tell you.
There were jars and jars of the good stuff, and no one to drink it.

15

Wrapped up in Yourself, You hid from me.
All day I looked for You
and when I found You hiding inside me,
I ran wild, playing now me, now You.

16

I came out, looking for the moon,
came looking, light flying to light.
All is Nārāyana! All is Nārāyana!
All is Nārāyana! Lord, You make my head spin.

17

(17 & 18 are companion vākhs)

Drifter, on your feet, get moving!
You still have time, go look for the Friend.
Make yourself wings, take wing and fly.
You still have time, go look for the Friend.

18

Charge your bellows with breath
like the blacksmith taught you.
That's how you turn your iron to gold.
You still have time, go look for the Friend.

19

(19 & 20 are companion *vākhs*)

Up, woman! Go make your offering.
Take wine, meat and a cake fit for the gods.
If you know the password to the Supreme Place,
you can reach wisdom by breaking the rules.

20

Fatten the five elements like they were rams meant for the sacrifice.
Feed them the grain of mind-light, and cakes fit for the gods.
Then kill them. But don't rush.
You need the password to the Supreme Place
to reach wisdom by breaking the rules.

21

Royal swan, what happened to your beautiful voice?
Someone's robbed you and you can't even say who or what.
The mill's stopped grinding, its mouth looks choked
and where's the grain? The miller's got clean away!

22

The mill goes round and round in slow circles
but the millstone guards its secret.
Sometimes, the wheel grinds closer to the grain,
sometimes, the grain rolls closer to the wheel.

23

What should I do with the five, the ten, the eleven
who scoured out this pot and ran away?
It's a numbers game: if all the eleven had pulled on their rope,
their cow wouldn't have gone astray.

24

You've got six and I've got six.
Now tell me, Blue-Throated One, what's the difference?
Or don't. I know. You keep your six on a leash
and my six have strung me along.

25

Lord! I've never known who I really am, or You.
I threw my love away on this lousy carcass
and never figured it out: You're me, I'm You.
All I ever did was doubt: Who am I? Who are You?

26

(This *vākh* has a double meaning)

Poor me, all helpless, I had to make a noise:
'I've got lotus stalks! Won't you buy some?'
I came back again and cried out loud:
'I've got onion and garlic! Two for the price of one!'

or

Poor me, all helpless, I had to make a noise:
'I've got nothing! Won't you buy some?'
I came back again and cried out loud:
'I've got breath and soul! Two for the price of one!'

27

(This *vākh* has a double meaning)

Onion and garlic are one, I've learnt.
Fry some onion. It's hardly a gourmet dish.
Fried onion, I wouldn't touch a sliver of it.
But it gave me a taste for saying 'I am He'.

or

Breath and soul, that's all I've learnt.
Worship your body, it tastes like nothing.
A body in worship, that's no way to bliss.
But it gave me a taste for saying 'I am He'.

28

Remove from my heart's dovecote, Father,
the ache for too-far skies.
My arms hurt from building other people's houses.
My body, when they come to take you from your own house,
a thousand people will follow you, waving their arms.
They'll lay you in a field, asleep on your right side,
head pointing south.

29

My soul is an elephant, an elephant that trumpets for food
every hour on the hour.
Out of a thousand, out of a hundred thousand, only one survives.
Thank God, or they'd have trampled all creation,
                                    these hungry tuskers.

30

You dance above the abyss.
How do you manage it?
You can't take these dishes with you when dinner's over.
Are you sure the buffet's tickling your palate?

31

I saw a sage starving to death, a leaf floating to earth
on a winter breeze. I saw a fool beating his cook.
And now I'm waiting for someone to cut
the love-cord that keeps me tied to this crazy world.

32

(32 & 33 are companion *vākhs*)

Now I see a flowing stream,
now a flood that's drowned all bridges,
now I see a bush flaming with flowers,
now a skeleton of twigs.

33

Now I see a blazing hearth,
now neither smoke nor fire,
now I see the mother of five princes,
now just the aunt of the potter's wife.

34

Bitter can be sweet and sweet poison.
It's a question of what your tongue wants.
It's hard work to tell what it wants, but keep going:
the city you're dreaming of, it's at the end of this road.

35

Master, my Master, listen to me!
Do you remember what the world was like?
Children, how will you pass your days and nights?
This is going to be one tough life.

36

There's bad news, and there's worse.
Autumn's pears and apples will ripen
with apricots in summer rain.
Mothers and daughters will step out,
hand in hand, in broad daylight, with strange men.

37

When day is snuffed out, the night glows.
The earth swells to touch the sky.
The new moon swallows the demon of eclipse.
Shiva is worshipped best when thought lights up the Self.

38

(38 & 39 are companion vākhs)

I, Lalla, set out to bloom like a cotton flower.
The cleaner tore me, the carder shredded me on his bow.
That gossamer: that was I
the spinning woman lifted from her wheel.
At the weaver's, they hung me out on the loom.

39

First the washerman pounded me on his washing stone,
scrubbed me with clay and soap.
Then the tailor measured me, piece by piece,
with his scissors. Only then could I, Lalla,
find the road to heaven.

40

You've cut yourself a hide and measured it
but what seed have you sown that will bear you fruit?
Fool! Teaching you is like throwing a ball at a gatepost
or feeding jaggery to an ox, hoping for milk.

41

Fool, you won't find your way out by praying from a book.
The perfume on your carcass won't give you a clue.
Focus on the Self.
That's the best advice you can get.

42

Don't flail about like a man wearing a blindfold.
Believe me, He's in here.
Come in and see for yourself.
You'll stop hunting for Him all over.

43

If you've learned how to bridle your breath,
hunger and thirst can't touch you.
Command your breath to the end
and you'll come back to earth, blessed.

44

You won't find the Truth
by crossing your legs and holding your breath.
Daydreams won't take you through the gateway of release.
You can stir as much salt as you like in water,
it won't become the sea.

45

I burnt the dirt from my mind,
twisted a knife in my heart,
spread my skirt to kneel at His door.
Only then did Lalla's name travel from mouth to mouth.

46

When the dirt was wiped away from my mind's mirror,
people knew me for a lover of God.
When I saw Him there, so close to me,
He was All, I was nothing.

47

As the moonlight faded, I called out to the madwoman,
eased her pain with the love of God.
'It's Lalla, it's Lalla,' I cried, waking up the Loved One.
I mixed with Him and drowned in a crystal lake.

48

I didn't believe in it for a moment
but I gulped down the wine of my own voice.
And then I wrestled with the darkness inside me,
knocked it down, clawed at it, ripped it to shreds.

49

I hacked my way through six forests
until the moon woke up inside me.
The sky's breath sang through me,
dried up my body's substance.
I roasted my heart in passion's fire
and found Shankara!

50

I pestled my heart in love's mortar,
roasted it and ate it up.
I kept my cool but you can bet I wasn't sure
whether I'd live or die.

51

My mind boomed with the sound of Om,
my body was a burning coal.
Six roads brought me to a seventh,
that's how Lalla reached the Field of Light.

52

I trapped my breath in the bellows of my throat:
a lamp blazed up inside, showed me who I really was.
I crossed the darkness holding fast to that lamp,
scattering its light-seeds around me as I went.

53

(53 & 54 are companion vākhs)

My Guru, Supreme Lord,
tell me the secret:
when both rise from the sun beneath the navel,
why does the short breath, coming out, cool,
and the long breath, coming out, burn?

54

The sun beneath the navel was made to burn.
When the breath, rising there, flows through the throat,
it comes out long and burns.
But when it meets the moon river flowing from the crown,
It comes out short and cools.

55

I came into this world of births and deaths
and found the true Self by mind-light.
No one will die for me, nor I for anyone.
How wonderful to die! How wonderful to live!

56

(This vākh has a double meaning)

I locked the doors of my body,
trapped the onion-thief and paused for breath.
Chaining him in my heart's dark cellar,
I stripped off his skin with the whip of Om.

or

I locked the doors of my body,
trapped the thief of life and held my breath.
Chaining him in my heart's dark cellar,
I stripped off his skin with the whip of Om.

57

A thousand times at least I asked my Guru
to give Nothingness a name.
Then I gave up. What name can you give
to the source from which all names have sprung?

58

God is stone, the temple is stone,
head to foot, all stone.
Hey priest-man, what's the object of your worship?
Get your act together, join mind with life-breath.

59

It covers your shame, keeps you from shivering.
Grass and water are all the food it asks.
Who taught you, priest-man,
to feed this breathing thing to your thing of stone?

60

Whoever chants Shiva's name as he walks the Swan's Way,
planting trees with no thought of the fruit,
even if the world keeps him busy night and day,
he's won the grace of the Teacher
who is First among the Gods.

61

Kusha grass, flowers, sesame seed, lamp, water:
it's just another list for someone who's listened,
really listened, to his teacher. Every day he sinks deeper
into Shambhu, frees himself from the trap
of action and reaction. He will not suffer birth again.

62

You are sky and earth,
day, wind-breath, night.
You are grain, sandal paste, flowers, water.
Substance of my offering, You who are All,
what shall I offer You?

63

He knows the crown is the temple of Self.
His breath is deepened by the Unstruck Sound.
He has freed himself from the prison of delusion.
He knows he is God, who shall He worship?

64

Whatever my hands did was worship,
whatever my tongue shaped was prayer.
That was Shiva's secret teaching:
I wore it and it became my skin.

65

Knowledge is a garden. Hedge it with calm,
self-restraint, right effort. Let your past acts graze in it,
goats fattened for the altars of the Mother Goddess.
When the garden is bare, the goats killed, you can walk free.

66

(66 & 67 are companion vākhs)

Who's the garland-maker, who's his wife?
What flowers will they pluck to offer Him?
With what water will they sprinkle Him?
With what chant will they wake the deepest Self?

67

The mind's the garland-maker, his wife the desire for bliss.
They will pluck flowers of adoration to offer Him.
They will sprinkle Him with the moon's dripping nectar.
They will wake the deepest Self with the chant of silence.

68

I, Lalla, came through the gate of my soul's jasmine garden
and found Shiva and Shakti there, locked in love!
Drunk with joy, I threw myself into the lake of nectar.
Who cares if I'm a dead woman walking!

69

Prune the weeds from your heart's garden
and the narcissus will bloom for you.
When you die, they'll want all your ledgers and journals.
Look out! Here comes Death, chasing you like a tax-collector.

70

(70 & 71 are companion vākhs)

I can't believe this happened to me!
A hoopoe cut off my claws with his beak.
The truth of all my dreams hit me in one line:
I, Lalla, find myself on a lake, no shore in sight.

71

I can't believe this happened to me!
I made a mess of everything, no shore in sight.
A klutz of a mason plastered my ceiling to the floor.
Serves me right: it's time I got to know myself.

72

He laughs when you laugh, sneezes in your sleep,
yawns for you, coughs for you.
He bathes every day in the river of your thoughts.
He's naked, all year round, and walks where you walk.
Just go up and introduce yourself.

73

When the sun melts away, the moon remains.
When the moon melts away, the mind remains.
When the mind melts away, what's left?
Earth, ether, sky, all empty out.

74

(74, 75 & 76 form a group of vākhs, sharing the same or near-identical closing line)

When the scriptures melt away, the chants remain.
When the chants melt away, the mind remains.
When the mind melts away, what's left?
A void mingles with the Void.

75

Kill desire, focus on the true nature of things.
Snap out of your daydreams,
there's rarest wisdom to be found right here.
A void has mingled with the Void.

76

I've bridled my mind-horse, reined him in,
struggled to tie my ten breath-streams together.
That's how the moon melted and rained nectar on me
and a void mingled with the Void!

77

My mind-horse straddles the sky,
crossing a hundred thousand miles in a blink.
It takes wisdom to bridle that horse,
he can break the wheels of breath's chariot.

78

(78 & 79 are companion vākhs)

Shiva's the horse and Vishnu's at the saddle,
Brahma's cheering at the stirrup.
Only the yogi, artful in breath and posture,
can say which god shall mount and ride this horse.

79

He who strikes the Unstruck Sound,
calls space his body and emptiness his home,
who has neither name nor colour nor family nor form,
who, meditating on Himself, is both Source and Sound,
is the god who shall mount and ride this horse.

80

Wear just enough to keep the cold out,
eat just enough to keep hunger from your door.
Mind, dream yourself beyond Self and Other.
Remember, this body is just pickings for jungle crows.

81

Gourmet meals and elegant clothes can't buy you peace of mind.
Only they climb higher, who have left delusion behind.
They know Death is fire behind a smiling mask
and Desire is a tough lender who talks sweet.

82

Gluttony gets you the best table in the town of Nowhere,
fasting gives your ego a boost.
Slave of extremes, learn the art of balance
and all the closed doors will open at your touch.

83

Now sir, make sure you've corralled your ass.
Or he'll champ his way
through your neighbours' saffron gardens.
No one's going to stand proxy
when it's your neck on the block.

84

Kill those killer ghouls, Lust, Anger and Greed,
before they can aim their arrows at your heart.
Armour yourself in thought, shield yourself with silence,
you'll soon see what they're really made of.

85

Kill those road pirates: Greed, Lust and Pride.
You'd be doing us all a great service.
And then you'll figure out how to reach the True Lord
and you'll see that the world is made of ash.

86

Your mind is the ocean of life.
It can throw up an angry tide
of fire-harpoons that stick in the flesh.
But weigh them, and they weigh nothing.

87

You're not happy ruling a kingdom,
you're not happy giving it away.
But if you're free of desire, you're free of dilemma.
Living, you're dead already, and can never die.

88

Whatever I've started, I'll finish.
But the accounts are someone else's headache.
Keep the reward, whatever I do is an offering to the Self.
Wherever I go, my only burden is lightness of step.

89

Train your thoughts on the path of immortality.
Leave them unguided and they'll grow
into monsters. But take heart, most of the time,
they're like children crying for milk.

90

Resilience: to stand in the path of lightning.
Resilience: to walk when darkness falls at noon.
Resilience: to grind yourself fine in the turning mill.
Resilience will come to you.

91

Good or bad, I'm happy to welcome both.
I don't hear with my ears, I don't see with my eyes.
A voice speaks inside my heart,
my jewel-lamp burns bright even in a rampaging wind.

92

They lash me with insults, serenade me with curses.
Their barking means nothing to me.
Even if they came with soul-flowers to offer,
I couldn't care less. Untouched, I move on.

93

Let them hurl a thousand curses at me,
pain finds no purchase in my heart.
I belong to Shiva. Can a scatter of ashes
ruin a mirror? It gleams.

94

Wisest to play the fool. Lynx-eyed, play blind.
Prick-eared, be deaf.
Polished, lie dull among the dull.
Survive.

95

My Master gave me just one rule:
Forget the outside, get to the inside of things.
I, Lalla, took that teaching to heart.
From that day, I've danced naked.

96

Want a kingdom? Raise a sabre.
Want heaven? Burn in penance, give to the poor.
Want knowledge of the Self? Listen to the Master.
Want your current balance of sin and virtue?
Better consult the Self.

97

Restless mind, don't infect the heart with fear.
That virus is not for you.
The Infinite knows what you hunger for.
Ask Him to carry you across.

98

(98, 99, 100, 101 & 102 form a group of vākhs, linked by their closing line)

They sprang in beauty from their mother's womb,
wounding it with their passage. Again and again,
they came back to wait at that door, but Shiva
can play hard to get: hold on to that message.

99

The stone of the temple is the stone of the paved road,
the stone that anchors the earth's continents
is the stone of the mill that can grind you down.
But Shiva can play hard to get: hold on to that message.

100

Does the sun not warm every country he visits
or does he touch only the richest ones?
Does water not flow in every house?
But Shiva can play hard to get: hold on to that message.

101

As mother, she suckles you. As wife, she pampers you.
As temptress, she puts a noose around your neck.
That's woman for you. But Shiva can play
hard to get: hold on to that message.

102

If only I'd trained my mind to gather my breath-streams,
played surgeon, cut and bound them, ground pain into
                                          an antidote,
I'd have known how to churn the Elixir of Life!
But Shiva can play hard to get: hold on to that message.

103

Pressed in winter's paws, running water hardens to ice
or powders into snow. Three different states
but the sun of wisdom thaws them down to one.
The world, all hands on board, has sunk without trace in Shiva!

104

Shiva lives in many places.
He doesn't know Hindu from Muslim.
The Self that lives in you and others:
that's Shiva. Get the measure of Shiva.

105

The Lord has spread the subtle net of Himself across the world.
See how He gets under your skin, inside your bones.
If you can't see Him while you're alive,
don't expect a special vision once you're dead.

106

You made a promise in the womb.
Will you keep it or won't you?
Die before death can claim you
and they will honour you when you go.

107

(107 & 108 are companion *vākhs*)

Who shall die, who shall be killed?
Who forgets the Name
and falls into the world's murky business:
he shall die, he shall be killed.

108

Who trusts his Master's word
and controls the mind-horse
with the reins of wisdom,
he shall not die, he shall not be killed.

109

Who sees Self as Other, Other as Self,
who sees day as night, night as day,
whose mind does not dance between opposites,
he alone has seen the Teacher
who is First among the Gods.

110

Alone, I crossed the Field of Emptiness,
dropping my reason and my senses.
I stumbled on my own secret there
and flowered, a lotus rising from a marsh.

111

What the books taught me, I've practised.
What they didn't teach me, I've taught myself.
I've gone into the forest and wrestled with the lion.
I didn't get this far by teaching one thing and doing another.

112

I gave myself to Him, body and soul,
became a bell that the clear note of Him rang through.
Thoughts fixed on Him, I flew through the sky
and unlocked the mysteries of heaven and hell.

113

You rule the earth, breathe life
into the five elements.
All creation throbs with the Unstruck Sound.
Immeasurable, who can take Your measure?

114

To the yogi, the whole wide world ripples into Nothingness:
it splashes like water on the water of Infinity.
When that Void melts, Perfection remains.
Hey priest-man, that's the only lesson you need!

115

Word or thought, normal or Absolute, they mean nothing here.
Even the mudrās of silence won't get you entry.
We're beyond even Shiva and Shakti here.
This Beyond that's beyond all we can name, that's your lesson!

116

Neither You nor I, neither object nor meditation,
just the All-Creator, lost in His dreams.
Some don't get it, but those who do
are carried away on the wave of Him.

117

New mind, new moon.
I've seen the great ocean made new.
Ever since I've scoured my body and mind,
I, Lalla, have been as new as new can be!

118

Reputation: it's water splashing in a creel.
Find me a hero who can trap a gale
in his fist, tether an elephant
with a hair. Maybe he'd dare
to hang on to reputation.

119

To dam a flood,
to blow out a forest fire,
to walk on air,
to milk a wooden cow:
any con artist could do it.

120

Who can halt the dripping frost
or cup the wind in his palms?
He can, who has reined in his five senses.
He can pluck the sun from the midnight sky.

121

He, from whose navel the First Syllable rises,
who crafts from his breath a bridge to heaven:
he carries just one mantra in his head,
why would he need a thousand spells?

122

Some run away from home, some escape the hermitage.
No orchard bears fruit for the barren mind.
Day and night, count the rosary of your breath,
and stay put wherever you are.

123

Hermit or householder: same difference.
If you've dissolved your desires in the river of time,
you will see that the Lord is everywhere and is perfect.
As you know, so shall you be.

124

Some, who have closed their eyes, are wide awake.
Some, who look out at the world, are fast asleep.
Some who bathe in sacred pools remain dirty.
Some are at home in the world but keep their hands clean.

125

Those who glow with the light of the Self
are freed from life even while they live.
But fools add knots by the hundred
to the tangled net of the world.

126

Don't waste your wisdom on a fool
or your sugar on an ass.
Don't plant seeds in the river's sand
or pour oil on bran cakes kept for the cow.

127

I can scatter the battalions of southern clouds,
dry the ocean, play physician
to the most lingering fever and cure it.
But I can't knock sense into a fool.

128

Master, leave these palm leaves and birch barks
to parrots who recite the name of God in a cage.
Good luck, I say, to those who think they've read the scriptures.
The greatest scripture is the one that's playing in my head.

129

It's so much easier to study than act,
to philosophise than go looking for the Self.
Losing the scriptures in the thick fog of my practice,
I stumbled on second sight.

130

This lake, even a mustard seed's too large to sink in it,
but everybody comes to drink its water.
Deer, jackals, rhinos, cloud-elephants are born,
and barely born, fall back into this lake.

131

Three times I saw a lake overflowing a lake.
Once I saw a lake mirrored in the sky.
Once I saw a lake that bridged
north and south, Mount Haramukh and Lake Kausar.
Seven times I saw a lake shaping itself into emptiness.

132

So many times I've drunk the wine of the Sindhu river.
So many roles I've played on this stage.
So many pieces of human flesh I've eaten.
But I'm still the same Lalla, nothing's changed.

133

Look out for Him.
He's played many roles on this stage.
Slough off envy, anger, hate.
Learn to take what you get.
You'll find Him.

134

We've been here before, we'll be here again,
we've been here since the birth of time.
The sun rises, sets, rises again.
Shiva creates, destroys, creates the world again.

135

(135 & 136 are companion vākhs)

Who's asleep and who's awake?
What is that lake in the sky
from which a rain of nectar is falling?
What is the offering that Shiva loves most?
What is that Supreme Word you're looking for
in the hermit's coded dictionary?

136

The mind's asleep. When it outgrows itself, it will awake.
The five organs are the lake in the sky
from which a rain of nectar is falling.
The offering Shiva loves most is knowledge of Self.
The Supreme Word you're looking for
is Shiva Yourself.

137

The chain of shame will break
if you steel yourself against jibes and curses.
The robe of shame will burn away
if you break in the mustang of your mind.

138

I prayed so hard my tongue got stuck to my palate
and still I couldn't worship You right.
My thumb and finger were sore from turning the rosary
and still my mind's phantoms wouldn't go away.

139

Don't torture this body with thirst and hunger,
give it a hand when it stumbles and falls.
To hell with all your vows and prayers:
just help others through life, there's no truer worship.

140

This body that you're fussing over,
this body that you're dolling up,
this body that you're wearing to the party,
this body will end as ash.

141

True mind, look inside this body,
this body they call the Self's own form.
Strip off greed and lust, polish this body,
this body as bright as the sun.

142

Don't think I did all this to get famous.
I never cared for the good things of life.
I always ate sensibly. I knew hunger well,
and sorrow, and God.

143

(143, 144, 145 & 146 form a group of *vākhs*, linked by their closing line)

A king's flywhisk, baldachin, chariot, throne,
pageants, evenings at the theatre, a downy bed.
Which of these will endure
or blot out the fear of death?

144

Delusion's captive, you threw yourself away like flotsam
on the ocean of life.
You broke the embankment
and fell into the marsh of shadows.
When Yama's warders come to drag you away bleeding,
who can blot out the fear of death?

145

You have two kinds of karma
and this dream-world has three tainted causes.
Destroy them all with your burning breath
and in the other world, they'll anoint you.
Up, use your wings, pierce the sun-disk.
It flies from you, the fear of death.

146

Wear the robe of wisdom,
brand Lalla's words on your heart,
lose yourself in the soul's light,
you too shall be free.

Notes to the Poems

These notes have been cast in the form of a detailed commentary. They are intended to provide an interpretation of the 146 *vākhs* of Lal Dĕd included in this translation, and to expand the reader's access to their content as well as their historical, philosophical and literary context. One of the specific aims of this section is to elucidate the images and conventions employed in Lalla's poetry, and to help clarify the sometimes obscure or occult meanings of *vākhs* that refer to concepts and practices associated with Yoga, Tantra and Kashmir Śaivism. These notes also annotate certain ideas and rituals mentioned in Lalla's poems which may seem alien or disconcerting to the contemporary Indian religious sensibility.

I have incorporated a concordance into these notes, instead of consigning it to a separate tabulation. Each note, accordingly, includes the corresponding *vākh* number from two benchmark collections: those of George Grierson and Lionel D. Barnett (1920) and Professor Jayalal Kaul (1973). Grierson and Barnett's numbering is indicated by a capital G, and Kaul's by a capital K. Where the *vākh* appears only in Grierson and Barnett, it carries a 'G' number; likewise, where it appears only in Kaul, it bears a 'K' number. Wherever a *vākh* has been taken from J. Hinton Knowles' *Dictionary of Kashmiri Proverbs and Sayings* (1885), or Knowles records a variant of that *vākh*, the note indicates this with a 'K. Pr' number.

Every note opens with the first line of the relevant *vākh*, rendered in Roman script with diacritical marks.

149

The proper names for the Divine, or of various deities, appear in diverse spellings throughout this text. For Shiva, to take a key example, I retain the spelling that is in common use, 'Shiva', in general contexts, but use the diacritically nuanced 'Śiva' in citing sources where it is so written; the Kashmiri original is rendered in Roman, depending on whether the usage is nominative or invocative, as 'Shiv' or 'Shiwa'.

I have varied the use of 'yogi' and 'yogini' throughout this section, to indicate that seekers belonging to both genders were engaged in the practices and the quest under review.

*

1. G: 36 | K: 108

prathuy tīrthan gatshān sannyās

2. K: 87

latan huṅd māz lāryōm vatan

These vākhs, 1 and 2, contain the kernel of Lal Děd's spiritual practice. Her concern is with inward and inner-directed evolution, not with the pursuit of shrines and pilgrimages, rituals and scriptures, observances and sacrifices. She argues that there is no reason to seek the Divine in places specially designated as holy, since the Divine, or the Self, is the core of one's own being. Parenthetically, we may note the scepticism expressed by many Indian mystic-poets towards pilgrimage sites, which often function as staging posts in an economy of faith that replaces the elusive possibilities of grace with the more tangible practicalities of commerce. The faraway grass of poem 1, the luxuriant *dramun*, is the *durva* grass used in Hindu rituals.

In poem 2, we find Lalla in her persona as the wanderer, intimate with the landscape and a stranger to domestic settings. Since the Divine pervades the universe, Lalla teaches, an experience of realisation or enlightenment is potentially available anywhere. As Joseph Campbell observes, in *The Hero with a Thousand Faces*: '[A] great temple can be established anywhere. Because, finally, the All is everywhere, and anywhere may become the seat of power. Any blade of grass may assume, in myth, the figure of the saviour and conduct the questing wanderer into the sanctum sanctorum of his own heart' (2008, 35).

The 'secret' that lies at the heart of wisdom teachings is usually a simple yet compelling and often ignored truth: here, it is the understanding of the omnipresence of the Divine, which Lalla distils from a 'hundred pieces of talk', from discourses and doctrines.

3. G: 8 | K: 73

Shiv wā Kěshěv wā Zin wā

Lal Děd adopts a variety of tones and attitudes towards the Divine, ranging from the offhand to the reverential, the lover's complaint to the questor's bemusement. Here, she fuses her longing for release from the 'sickness of life', *bhawa-ruz*, with the teaching that the particularisation of the Divine into a deity by various religious lineages has little use unless it can cure the questor of this fundamental affliction. The alternatives that Lalla offers in this poem indicate the religious landscape of Kashmir in the fourteenth century: the Divine is Shiva or *Shiv*, the Auspicious One, to the Śaivites; Vishnu or *Kěshěv*, the Killer of the Demon Keshi, to the Vaishnavites; the Buddha or Zin, the Conqueror, to the Buddhists; and Brahma or Kamal-aza-nāth, the Lotus-born Lord, to his devotees. Lalla refers to the Buddha as Zin, from the Sanskrit Jina, meaning one who has conquered the senses and desires, and overcome the cycle of rebirth: an appellation evidently used at that date to designate both the Buddha and Mahavira, although later and elsewhere applied only to Mahavira.

4. G: 106 | K: 1

āmi pana sŏdaras nāvi chĕs lamān

Lal Dĕd employs an image beloved of the saint-poets of India: the self as a boat tossed about on the ocean of life. Her image adds a layer of complication, since the boat is being towed: here, as in several other poems, Lalla uses the image of the river boat being towed by labourers or horses on a tow-path. And when the river boat goes out into the ocean, as it is shown to do here, there is no tow-path from which it can be guided: poem 4 spells out a trope of hazard and impossibility. The second image in the poem is also one popular with India's saint-poets: the body as a leaky vessel. The closing line presents the questor as wanderer, lost and far away from home, indeed with no knowledge of where home might lie. Of interest, here, is the play of scale through which the image of water is presented as both epic/external and intimate/internal: the self, visualised as a boat on the ocean in the first two lines of the vākh, becomes water itself in the next two lines, in danger of seeping away from the half-baked cup of the body.

5. G: 67 | K: 2

lalith lalith waday bŏ-döy

This poem records a classic moment in the early phase of the journey towards spiritual realisation: the recognition that the soul has been held hostage by the world of appearances, variously glossed in the Sanskrit tradition as mithyā or māyā. The questor must free the self from the illusion that the world, with its objects and experiences, is permanent. To forget who you are is to forget the true path and purpose of the Self, which is enlightenment, the act of finding again the lost way home, which recurs in Lalla's poems. The iron anchor, lŏh-langar, is an image drawn from the nautical life of Kashmir's lakes and rivers: it signifies the things of the world, the attachments that keep us moored in the world of appearances, and which, Lalla suggests, will not accompany the self on the onward journey after death.

6. G: 98 | K: 5 | K. Pr: 18 (variant)

āyĕs watē gayĕs na watē

This poem may be read in two different ways. It opens with the image of two roads: the first is the natural process of birth by which the bodied self is born, without choice and carrying the baggage of previous lives; and the other, the way by which it leaves the world, death transformed from an inevitable event into a willed and perfected choice to release oneself from the cycle of rebirth. The word *wath* means both a physical path and a spiritual way. Accordingly, the action of the poem takes place at a threshold moment charged with considerable allusive power, hinting at the possibility of a transformative experience: twilight surprises the speaker just as she is about to cross a river.

The poem itself takes two roads: we are cued to its doubleness of meaning by the difference between an oral and a scribal rendition of a key term in the second line, *suman-sŏthi-manz*. If read as *suman*, this term indicates that the speaker stands on a broken embankment partially restored by means of makeshift plank-bridges. The pronunciation of this artisanal word is identical, however, with the more cultivated *sŏman*, from the Sanskrit *sva-man*: one's own mind. An associated difference between the oral and the scribal occurs in the third line: the word *hār* or cowrie can be read as *Har* or Shiva.

Depending on which combination we prefer, *suman* + *hār* or *sŏman* + *Har*, the poem functions either as a lament on the travails of everyday life, or as an esoteric account of a spiritual crisis. The speaker may have been surprised by twilight on an embankment in disrepair, caught short of travel money; or she may stand on the precarious embankment of her own mind, aware that she has not developed the necessary reserves of meditative energy to embark on the next stage in her journey.

The figure of the ferryman suggests the myth of the soul's perilous journey across the river Vaitarni after death. As in similar myths found in ancient Egypt and Greece, Hindu mythology also equipped the soul with a coin for the ferryman, to ease the discomforts of transit: the cowrie that Lalla finds she does not possess, the talisman of Shiva's name.

7. G: 107 | K: 15

hā manashě! kyāzi chukh wuṭhān sěki-lawar

Here, as in *vākh* 16, the Divine is invoked as Nārān or Nārāyana, a name of Vishnu. This may appear surprising, given Lalla's affiliation with Kashmir Śaivism, but she uses the names of Shiva and Vishnu interchangeably. As we have seen in poem 3, she is not overly preoccupied with sectarian conceptions of the Divine.

Like many of Lalla's poems, this one takes its images from Kashmir's riverine economy. The speaker scoffs gently at the man who—in the spirit of the wise men of Gotham or the denizens of the *Narrenschiff*, the Ship of Fools so prominent in mediaeval European folklore—twists a rope from sand. Another of Lalla's tropes of impossibility, this symbolises the belief in a worldly life, which is foredoomed in her view. The only course along which the self can navigate, sings Lalla, is the one that discloses itself when the individual self overcomes its separation from the Divine.

8. G: 19 | K: 7

atshĕn āy ta gatshun gatshē

Lalla offers a bleak vision of the world's inhabitants in this poem, as transients who are born only to die, who die only to be reborn. The piquant cadence of the closing line conveys the measure of this dance of perpetual circularity: *kĕh na-ta kĕh na-ta kĕh na-ta kyāh*. This vision may appear unremittingly nihilistic if read outside the context of Lalla's spiritual convictions: to her, these souls are trapped in the cycle of rebirth, and must redeem themselves by making the effort of self-perfection.

9. G: 41 | K: 8

āyĕs kami dishi ta kami watē

This poem addresses, as poem 6 does, the theme of the two roads: birth and death; choiceless arrival in the world, and a shaped and perfected departure from it. In expressing the fear that she may waste her life without having developed, literally, a sense of direction, Lalla records yet another phase of the spiritual life: that of momentary doubt and self-doubt, and an appeal to the Divine to send help. The poems of Lal Děd, like those of many questors, are veined through with the perception that life is a precious opportunity for the achievement of perfection, which could be wasted through inattention or ignorance.

10. G: 108 | K: 23

nābá di-bāras aṭ a-gaṇḍ ḍyolu gōm

The pastoral images of this poem evoke the landscape of rural Kashmir. It describes a moment of awakening: the questor, having ignored her teacher's advice and chosen the path of worldly life, realises that it is a wrong turn. The sack of candy that she carries suggests the pleasures of material life, suddenly devoid of attraction. Lalla's poems compress great metaphorical energy, which is released when the utterance transfers itself from one domain of images to another: here, the self, imaged as the lost traveller in the first two lines, becomes the scattered flock of the last line, a diffused array of faculties and emotions that needs the well-guided mind to gather it into coherence.

11. G: 48 | K: 74

Lal bŏh lūtshüs tshāḍan ta gwāran

Lalla recalls the rigours of the spiritual quest, when her wanderings seemed futile and the door of grace was shut against her. At the end of this stretching of human potentiality to its utmost, she says, she found a reserve of power of whose existence she had not been aware. This is an experience that mystics as well as athletes record; and in some deep sense, as is evident from the sheer physicality of her language of spiritual effort, Lalla is an athlete of self-overcoming. She focuses her love, purified and strengthened by the tests of her endurance, on the Divine—which manifests Itself to her.

12. K: 4

hacivi horinji pětsiv-kān gom

In this enigmatic poem, which unfolds in an urban setting replete with archery meadow, palace, marketplace and waterside shrine, Lalla speaks of the self that is not yet fully prepared to set out on the quest. Skill and aim, intention and execution, dream and reality, timing and desired event, all pass one another by, leaving the self frustrated and helpless. I would go a step further and read the ill-equipped archer, the clumsy carpenter, the feckless shopkeeper and the ritually impure devotee as representing the four *varnas* or castes of the classical Hindu social order: the warrior, the artisan, the trader and the priest. Since none seems able to serve his *svadharma*, or the duty prescribed for him by his birth-caste in the Bhagavad Gita account, the self is visualised here as having passed into a space of being and self-knowledge that is beyond society: the individual who has embraced the questor's life is no longer able to function within society's net of norms and expectations.

13. G: 3 | K: 97

Lal bǒh drāyěs lōla rě

As in poem 11, Lalla recounts the progress of the passionate quest. Once again, the quest is presented as a returning curve: crazed by the love of God, the questor goes out into the field of experience but returns to the space of the self, finding at home what she thought to find in the world, in intimate proximity what she believed to be at a great distance. The figure sought for in this poem is not the Divine, however, but the 'teacher': the master or sage who appears in a number of Lalla's vākhs, and is thought to refer to her spiritual guide, Siddha Śrīkāntha.

14. G: 60 | K: 99

tshāḍān lūtshüs pōnī-pānas

This poem carries the metaphor of restless search into inner space: Lalla realises that she must look, not for One outside, but for herself. But the intellectual realisation of the identity of self and Self, by means of *jñāna-mārga*, must be sustained and actualised through the exercise of *bhakti-mārga*. She finds secret knowledge, which admits her into a zone that she describes as *al-thān*, the place of wine, which may be interpreted as symbolically denoting the *sahasrāra chakra*, the 'thousand-petalled' centre in the brain region, which is visualised in Yoga as a moon that drips nectar. One of the aims of Yoga is the activation of this centre, which produces an experience of enlightenment and release. This nectar or wine of enlightenment is potentially available to all bodied selves, suggests Lal Dĕd, but very few apprentice themselves to the wisdom lineages that could prepare them to drink it.

15. G: 44 | K: 137

pānas lōgith rūdukh mĕ tsah

16. G: 109 | K: 128

ạndariy āyĕs tsạndariy gārān

In these poems, Lalla employs the metaphor of the game or *līla* as it is known in Sanskrit, to suggest the now-playful now-melancholy exchanges between questor and Divine. In poem 15, she presents self and Self as playing a game of hide and seek, with the twist that each is concealed in the other. When the identity of self and Self is discovered, the game of mutual concealment gives way to celebration. The questor gains the freedom to switch at will between her normal role in the world and her true identity as one who has tasted the nectar of enlightenment.

Poem 16 maps the metaphor of the game over a Yogic account of the activation of the *kuṇḍalinī-śakti* or energy, which culminates in the opening of the *sahasrāra* spoken of in poem 14 (Singh 1979c, 25–28). Lalla emerges from within her soul to receive the enlightenment of the nectar moon, and discovers that the world is saturated with the presence of the Divine, here invoked (as in poem 7) as Nārān, Nārāyana or Vishnu, and that all creation has been produced by his play.

17. G: 99

gŏphilo! haka kadam tul

18. G: 100 | K. Pr: 46 (variant incorporating elements of both 17 and 18)

daman-basti ditō dam

These companion *vākhs*, which have been in popular circulation in Kashmir in the remembered past, are of an appreciably late date from their use of Persianate phrases. Indeed, these two poems, as well as poem 69, are quatrains 'that belong to one Azizullah Khan (early 19th century) [and] ascribed to Lal Děd', as S.S. Toshkhani points out in his paper, 'Reconstructing and Reinterpreting Lal Děd' (2002, 60–61). Nonetheless, poems 17 and 18 were included by Grierson in his 1920 edition, which records a line of transmission that begins with the oral recitation of Pandit Dharma-dāsa Darwēsh, which was scribally rendered for Grierson by his associate Mahāmahopādhyāya Pandit Mukunda Rāma Sāstrī in 1914. Meanwhile, nearly three decades earlier, the Rev. J. Hinton Knowles had included a text incorporating elements of both 17 and 18 in his *Dictionary of Kashmiri Proverbs and Sayings* (1885), commenting that these were '[a] few lines from Lal Děd constantly quoted by the Kashmiri' (reproduced in Grierson and Barnett 1920, 123).

It is not impossible that these widely circulated Azizullah poems, presented even by Pandit reciters as songs by Lalla, may register a comparatively recent version, or update if you will, of material from what I have called the LD corpus in my Introduction, originally circulating in an earlier form of Kashmiri. As I have argued in the Introduction, I am willing to set aside the question of judgement on material that is deemed corrupt or an interpolation, since, in my account, the LD corpus is the outcome of multiple intersections among contributors: reciters, scribes, redactors, archivists and commentators.

The speaker in poems 17 and 18 summons the lazy, aimless or reluctant soul to action, spurring it to recognise that there still remains a brief opportunity to rise beyond the limitations of the ordinary life, to embrace the spiritual path and to 'go look for the Friend'. While the imagery of the charged bellows suggests Yoga, where it refers to the science of controlling the vital breaths that course through the body's channels, the motif of the transmutation of iron into gold indicates the influence of *rasāyana-shāstra*, the Indian tradition of gnosis through alchemy; the use of the Persianate term *yār* or Friend to denote the Divine marks the unmistakeable impress of Sufi usage.

19. G: 10

wŏth rainyā! artsun sakhar

20. G: 77 | K: 60

mŏrith pŏnts būth tim phal-handī

In these companion poems, which are in the nature of soliloquies, Lalla gathers the courage to take an irrevocable step, leaving the norm-governed world of householders behind and entering a world of secret rituals of illumination and heterodox practices of ecstasy. In poem 19, she is Shakti to Shiva, the feminine principle to the male, the female worshipper playing her role in the rituals of *Kulācāra*, the Kaula school, or the Tantric underground of mediaeval Kashmir, as I have termed it in my Introduction.

This Tantric underground forms part of the pan-Indian movement described, by scholars, as the *vāma-mārga*, the 'left-hand path of enlightenment', which allows the well-guided and ritually prepared questor to 'reach wisdom by breaking the rules'. Kaula ritual variously deploys meat, wine and sexual union between initiates not bound by marriage vows, as instruments by which to overcome the inhibitions of normality, to propel the self beyond the polarities and differentiations of a social and psychic life conditioned by convention, and towards a receptiveness to illumination.

The five elements referred to in poem 20 are the five constituents of the universe or *pancha-mahā-bhūtas*: that is, bhū, earth or solidity; *āpa*, water or liquidity; *agni*, fire or formative energy; *vayū*, air or aeriality; and *ākāsa*, ether or emptiness. The logic of the poem proposes that these five elements must be fattened for the sacrifice, that is, meditated upon and explored through contemplation until they have lost the illusion of power and reality that they impose on the consciousness; only then can the grip of the universe fade from the mind. However, the process is a delicate one, and any false step or missed stage can condemn the failed questor to delusional arrogance, a fragmented consciousness, or worse, states of impaired consciousness. Also, without the guidance of a guru and the presence of the Divine, Kaula practices could easily degenerate into sensual gratification. Hence the caveat that one still needs the password: the personal mantra, passed on by guru to disciple in a whisper and never to be written down, *alekhya*, which governs and stabilises the process by which the self must break itself and its matrix of normality down, in order to renew itself.

21. G: 86 | K: 107

rāza-hams ösith sapodukh koluy

I would read this poem as combining playfulness and melancholia, in its evocation of the gains and losses attendant upon the gift of beatitude. A deep serenity wells up from within the questing self, silencing the melodious eloquence that formerly distinguished it; the life of ceaseless activity has been renounced in favour of stillness. The royal swan has been robbed of its voice and the mill has been choked, although mysteriously, since nothing impedes it, and the grain is missing: the voice-thief and the absconding miller are one, the Divine.

22. K: 56

gratu chu phērān ze ri zerē

The 'secret' central to all wisdom teachings, as simple in the telling as it is difficult in the doing, appears here as the shifting and unpredictable balance between labour and grace, the questor's effort and the unprompted abundance of the Divine. The mill symbolises the slow, sustained rhythms of spiritual practice; the grain is the self, and the wheel is the Self.

23. G: 95 | K: 6

kyāh kara pŏntsan dahan ta kāhan

Numeric lists of symbolic import, such as the one that underwrites the action of poem 23, recur in the poems and fables of India's mystics, adepts and saints. These remain open to a variety of interpretations, and there are often as many interpretations as there are commentators. The most compelling reading of this poem is that the numbers that appear in it, taken together, propose an image of the human body as the sum of diverse and normally divergent energies. The 'five' are the *pancha-mahā-bhūtas*, already met with and accounted for in poem 20. The 'ten' are the principal and secondary vital breaths coursing within the body, in the Yogic system. The 'eleven' are the *jñānēndriya*, the five organs of sense perception, and the *karmēndriya*, the five organs of action, taken together with *manas*, the governing faculty of intelligence.

The bodied self is visualised in the first two lines of the poem as a pot that has had all its food scraped away by opportunists who have taken their chance and fled; and in the last two lines, as a cow that has escaped because its eleven masters could not cooperate to pull it in the same direction. As in other poems where Lalla shifts the relative scale and valency of images, the shift of metaphorical energy here presents the self first as presence and then as absence: first as a pot left behind by its users, and then as a cow that has escaped, leaving its fractious masters behind.

24. G: 13 | K: 129

yimąy shĕh tsĕ timąy shĕh mĕ

Shiva is addressed here, quite informally, as *Shyāma-galā*, 'Blue-throated One', from the Sanskrit appellation, *Nīlkaṇṭha*. Only the fear of an unintended echo of Deep Throat, with its associations with American pornography and internal espionage, prevented me from rendering Lalla's address here as the more direct, 'Now tell me, Blue-throat, what's the difference?' Shiva came to possess this anatomical attribute because he swallowed a deadly poison, the *halāhala*, which was thrown up when the gods and demons joined to churn the Ocean of Milk to draw up the nectar of immortality, the *amrita*. In saving the world from the toxicity of *halāhala*, Shiva placed himself at risk: forever after, he held the poison in his throat, which turned blue, a marked contrast against his pale, ash-smeared body. A symbol of Shiva's gesture as saviour, the blue throat is also a token of his ability to control his faculties, command circumstances and withstand all negativity.

Indian mystical literature permits considerable latitude to the interpreter, at least partly because India's spiritual traditions teach that true meaning eludes the probing intellect while it rewards meditative awareness, that it resides in the non-discursive realm of meaning at the borderlands of language. When in doubt about the exact nature of a numeric list of symbolic import, as in poem 23, pick your own. Here, extending George Grierson's speculations (1920, 35), I would suggest that Shiva's 'six' are the attributes of the Supreme Deity, namely eternity, omniscience, omnipotence, absolute tranquillity, absolute self-sufficiency and the ability to reside beyond form while manifesting Itself at will. Lalla's 'six', meanwhile, may well signify the weaknesses of the unreconstructed human self, namely lust, anger, greed, arrogance, delusion and envy, some of which appear elsewhere in the LD corpus.

25. G: 7 | K: 130

nātha! nā pān nā par zônum

Lalla phrases a passionate testament, here, to the recognition of the unity between seeker and goal, self and Self. She castigates herself for having allowed herself to be blinded to this unity by her body-centred consciousness, with its emphasis on the personality, on individual identity; and also by the constant doubt concerning the true nature of the Divine, which she previously nurtured.

26. G: 89

lācāri bicāri prawād korum

The double meaning of this *vākh* hinges on the alternative meanings carried by three of the key words: *nadoru*, which means both 'lotus stalk' and 'a thing of no value'; *prān*, which means both 'onion' and the 'life-breath'; and *ruhun*, which means 'garlic' and puns on *ruh* or spirit, a word derived from the Arabic. The opening line is a vivid study in the illuminating paradox at which Lalla excels. Describing herself, somewhat disarmingly, as a poor and helpless woman, she makes a proclamation: *lācāri bicāri prawād korum*. In the first reading, she offers lotus stalks for sale—*nadoru*, stewed either by itself or with meat, is a favourite Kashmiri dish—following this up with an offer of onion and garlic at a discounted price. The second, more esoteric understanding plays off this sales patter at a deeper level: the 'nothing' that Lalla pitches at the prospective buyer in the marketplace gains significance when she follows it up by offering 'breath and soul' for the price of one. What is on offer is Yogic instruction, and through it, the resulting insight into the Void, the true nature of reality beyond the world of appearances.

27. G: 90

prān ta ruhun kunuy zônum

This *vākh* also employs the pun on onion/life-breath and garlic/spirit. Depending on how it is read, the poem is spoken either by a fastidious yet idiosyncratic gourmand or an enlightened seeker. The gourmand speaks urbanely of how he wouldn't touch a sliver of fried onion, but that it gave him, nonetheless, a taste for the mystical realisation, 'sō-'ham', 'I am He'. The seeker arrives at the same conclusion by means of the pun that we have seen in play in poem 26: breath and soul form the twin subject of his training; he disdains the worship of the body, but agrees that it gave him a taste for saying 'sō-'ham', 'I am He'. The point of the double meaning appears to be that one may choose many, sometimes surprising and apparently mutually exclusive, ways to reach enlightenment, and the aesthete or epicurean may arrive at that destination just as surely as the ascetic.

28. K. Pr: 57

diluku khura-khura mě, Māli, kāstam, manaki kōtar-marē

In a recognition of the burden of the seeker's responsibility, Lalla implores the Divine to rid her of the longing for transcendence, and also of the mandate to care for the spiritual well-being of others. Contemplating her own death, she uses the imagery of the Hindu funeral: the procession, attended by crowds of mourning votaries; the body laid on its right side, with its head towards the south, which is the auspicious home of gods and angels, the quarter whose guardian or dik-pāla is Yama, the Lord of Death.

29. K. Pr: 150

naphsüy myônu chuy hostuy, ámi hásti mongunam gari gari bal

This poem invokes a terrifying vision of the unregenerate self as an insatiably hungry elephant: one that must be fed hourly if it is to be kept out of mischief. The speaker builds on the belief, common to the Hindu, Buddhist and Jaina traditions, that human birth is relatively rare; so that there are comparatively few of these tuskers in existence, or else they would have destroyed the universe with their rampaging desires. Significantly, though, the word that designates 'soul' in this poem is the Perso-Arabic *naphs*, which is also used colloquially and in the Unani medical system to mean pulse, subtle breath or true nature: its use clearly identifies poem 29 as a contribution to the LD corpus from a source oriented towards Sufi practice. In the Koran, the *naphs* is regarded as the lower or bestial nature, which the higher nature must refine, neutralise and overcome through a process of self-purification involving meditation, prayer, rigorous psychological analysis and a turning away from the gratifications of the material world. In the teachings of Kashmir's Rishi order, as epitomised in the *śruks* of Nund Rishi, *naphs* can mean both 'self' and 'ego': the aspirant is constantly urged to purify his *naphs*, to polish it like a mirror so that it can reflect the glory of transcendent knowledge.

30. K: 3

talu chuy zyus tay pĕṭhu chuk natsān

In this poem, Lalla satirises those who have devoted themselves to sensual pleasures, to the dance and the feast: but death will put an end to the feast, and the dance of life unfolds above the abyss of extinction.

31. G: 83 | K: 9

gāṭulwāh akh wuchum bŏcha-sūty marān

Lalla expresses, in this poem, her exasperation in the face of the world's inexplicable cruelty and manifest injustice, the transience of all that was loved and cherished: a wise man may die of hunger; a cook may be brutally mistreated by his whimsical master; the bright leaves of spring will be stripped off the trees in winter. And yet she both hates and loves this world, and hopes that a miraculous surgery of wisdom may sever the umbilical cord that keeps her attached to it.

32. G: 96 | K: 10

dámiy ḍiṭhüm nad wahawüñüy

33. G: 97 | K: 11 | K. Pr: 47

(variant incorporating elements of both 32 and 33)

dámiy ḍiṭhüm güjü dazawüñüy

These companion vākhs offer testimony to the transitory character of the world in a manner that is visually arresting: indeed, the poems develop as visual sequences edited at a pace that we would recognise as contemporary, more cinematic than imagistic. In poem 32, the speaker first sees a stream, an impression erased by the image of a deluge, then a flowering bush, quickly replaced by the same bush denuded by winter. In poem 33, the speaker reports a flourishing hearth, then the erasure of the hearth, succeeded by a vision of Kunti, sometime queen of Hastinapur and mother of the royal Pāndava brothers, replaced seamlessly by a humble figure, the aunt of the potter's wife. The last sequence refers to the episode in the Mahabharata when the five Pāndavas and their mother have been exiled by their cousins, the Kauravas, and spend part of that exile in disguise.

In the canonical version of the Mahabharata, the princes camouflage themselves as poor Brahmins; in this version, they would appear to have disappeared into an artisanal milieu. It should be noted, in this context, that the reference to the potter's wife may be a vestigial citation of the Tantric underground, whose nocturnal practices deliberately transgressed the caste lines of daytime society. Indeed, the potter's wife is a key figure, acting as a liberating sexual partner to the yogi, in one of the forms of the circle sacrifice or *chakra-yāga*, which features among the secret rituals of the Kaula adepts of Kashmir (Dupuche 2003, 128).

34. K: 20

ţyŏţh mŏdhur tay myūţh zahr

Lalla comments on the bewilderments of experience in this poem, and the deceptiveness of sensual impressions: one cannot even trust oneself. Only an adherence to one's chosen purpose can help one navigate through life, sifting one's true choices from the plenitude of illusions. At the end of this challenging road lies the city of redemption.

35. G: 91

Siddha-Māli! Siddhō! sĕda kathan kan thāv

36. G: 92

brŏţh-kŏli āsan tithiy kĕran

In these two poems, Lalla predicts the shape of things to come, and it is not encouraging. She laments the loss of more innocent and serene times, and foresees the coming of disasters: deprivation faces the children to come; changes in the weather pattern will play havoc with the fruiting seasons; mothers and daughters will join each other in consorting with strangers. Semaphoric of social unrest, Lalla's prognostications in poems 35 and 36 find disturbing fulfilment in the continuing turbulence in contemporary Kashmir, with its lethal combination of insurgency, low-intensity proxy warfare, militant terror and State repression.

37. G: 22

děn tshězi ta razan āsē

Lalla, as a fully realised yogini, testifies here to the expansion of consciousness that she experiences: the conventional distinction between bright day and dark night collapses, and the night finds its own luminosity; the horizon fades away, so that the earth loses its boundaries and merges with the sky. The resplendent new moon, symbolic of the awakened mind, swallows Rahu, the demon of eclipse, instead of being swallowed by him; the finest way of worshipping Shiva is not through rituals and observances, but through the knowledge-radiant mind (Singh 1979c, 103–05).

38. G: 102 | K: 105

Lal bŏh drāyĕs kapasi-pōshĕcĕ sütsüy

39. G: 103 | K: 106

dŏbi yĕli chŏvünas dŏbi-kañĕ-pĕṭhạy

The interpretation of these exquisite and poignant companion *vākhs* has varied considerably. While Grierson favours an account of 'various stages towards the attainment of knowledge . . . metaphorically indicated' (1920, 114), Jaishree Kak treats these poems as evidence of Lalla's 'trials and tribulations [as] a woman in mediaeval society', 'her awareness of the social construction of gender', 'the shredding of [her] old identity', and her transcendence of 'the socially defined 'feminine' self, which she experiences as oppressive' (2007, 5–7).

As I read it, Lalla's hope of blooming like the cotton flower incarnates the wish to attain the state that the mystics call *sahaja* in Sanskrit, or *sahaz* in Kashmiri: the awareness of one's true nature, the reality concealed by the world of appearances. This is not, however, a wish easily granted: before that, her body-centred consciousness, her sense of personality, must be beaten out of her. The imagery of these poems is that of violent, even brutal transformation: the seeker is torn and shredded, spun out into fine filaments, hung on the loom, woven, pounded, washed and cut to measure. The bodied self that she was is taken apart completely and subjected to remaking: it is only by suffering this process that she can 'find the road to heaven'.

The various artisans who are the protagonists of these poems—the cleaner, the carder, the spinning woman, the weaver, the washerman and the tailor—are all agents of transcendence. I would see them as guru, master or teacher figures, or as those mysterious 'helpers', demigods or guardian angels assigned by God to protect the seeker-hero or -heroine, who populate fables and wisdom stories across the world. Instructively, given my speculations about the trans-caste character of mediaeval Kashmir's Tantric underground, these pivotal catalyst figures in the process of spiritual evolution are all drawn from the labouring castes.

40. G: 66 | K: 16

tsarmun tsaṭith ditith pǎni pānas

Lalla derides the individual who is attached to the pleasures of the flesh, satirising the body as a mere hide, a dead possession. By contrast, she asks why he has not sown seeds that would bring in a harvest, the blessing of life and prosperity. As a teacher, Lalla often demarcates the limits of instruction, realistically defining the act of dispelling incorrigible folly as wasted effort. Here, as images of wasted effort, she deploys the ball that rebounds when thrown at a gatepost, and the absurd feeding of an ox with jaggery, which is correctly fed to a cow to increase her milk.

41. K: 59

mūḍō kriy chay na dārun ta pārun

In the same vein as poem 40, Lalla rebukes the fool who goes to extremes, believing he can find salvation by praying formulaically or wasting his life in the pursuit of voluptuary enjoyment. 'Focus on the Self' is her recommendation.

42. K: 50

kavu chukh divān anine batsh

Lalla remonstrates, in this poem, with the individual who seeks the Divine everywhere, without being able to see that enlightenment lurks in every corner of the universe: such a seeker is effectively blind to illumination, but Lalla proposes to shake him free of delusion.

43. G: 37 | K: 51

pawan pūrith yusu ani wagi

The bridling of the breath or *pūraka* is a Yogic technique, and an essential element of *prāṇāyāma*, the discipline of the body's vital breaths, which is an important step in the journey towards union with the Divine. One who has mastered this technique is liberated from hunger and thirst; he will be born again, only to release himself from the cycle of birth and death.

44. G: 29 | K: 76

sahazas shěm ta dam nō gatshi

In this crisp, no-nonsense poem, Lalla teaches that enlightenment cannot be achieved if the seeker merely practices asceticism as routine rather than as inspired practice. He will accomplish nothing if the fervency of his desire for transcendence is not matched by the strenuous effort of understanding and modulating the body's latencies, and the mastery of the techniques of right mindfulness. A simulation can never substitute for the reality or desired achievement that it simulates.

45. G: 49 | K: 86

mal wǒndi zōlum

While all of Lal Děd's *vākhs* are inherently and intensely autobiographical to a considerable degree, dwelling more on the rhythm of the spiritual journey than on the details of personal life, some of her poems can dwell on specific moments of experience: peak experiences during which the distinction between the personal and the spiritual life is dissolved, and when, so to speak, the spiritual becomes the personal for the questor, and no longer a matter of textual learning or abstraction. In poem 45, the vibrancy of her voice edged with violent feeling, Lalla describes how she purified her consciousness, refined her reason, senses and emotions, cultivated patience and humility, and so received the gift of illumination at the door of the Self. Only after going through this transfiguring experience did she become truly known as Lalla, and her reputation spread.

46. G: 31 | K: 100

makuras zan mal tsolum manas

Similar in spirit to poem 45, this poem celebrates the cleaning of the 'doors of perception', in William Blake's memorable phrase. With her mind's mirror cleansed of all dirt, Lalla became known as a votary of the Divine, a mystic with teachings to communicate. And yet, she became more aware than ever of how her individual personality was as nothing before the sublime majesty of the Divine.

47. G: 105 | K: 88

polu zūni wŏthith motu bōlanôwum

Lalla plays among personae in this poem: she is the madwoman, and she is the one who brings ease to the madwoman with the love of God. She awakens and joins with the Loved One, who is the Self: this process of union marks the falling away of all karmic defilements and the attainment of an indescribable clarity of being.

48. G: 104 | K: 92

sütsüsas na sātas pütsüsas na rumas

Poem 48 is characterised, as many of the *vākhs* are, by violent imagery. Lalla begins by recalling her own doubts about her poetry, despite which she 'gulped down the wine' of her *vākhs*. These manifestos of illumination gave her the strength to face the demons and monsters haunting her own soul, the 'darkness inside' that she confronts and does battle with, in the spirit of Jacob wrestling all night with the Angel in the Old Testament, or Gilgamesh battling Humbaba, or Greek heroes such as Perseus and Jason fighting various dragons to liberate the imprisoned young woman or the hidden treasure symbolising emancipatory wisdom held in reserve. Significantly, Lalla's choices of verb are physical, visceral, robust and redolent of the hero's quest: she wrestles with the darkness inside herself, knocks it down, claws at it, rips it to shreds.

49. G: 25 | K: 93

shĕ wan tsaṭith shĕshi-kal wuzüm

50. K: 75

loluki vŏkhalu wāliṅj piśim

I have clustered, as poems 49–56, *vākhs* in which Lalla elaborates a number of interrelated metaphors that refer closely to Yogic techniques of breath control. In poem 49, the journey through the six forests and the waking up of an inner moon refer to the yogini's practice of raising her *kuṇḍalinī* energy through six *chakras* or centres of energy within the body, charted broadly along the spine, and then further up to the *sahasrāra*, the nectar moon associated with the brain. Once the six *chakras* have been mastered, the initiate masters the art of looking at and past the material universe. And once the inner moon has been activated, the vital breaths within the body modulated into coordination, the body's energies brought into harmony, and the self impelled by the love of the Divine, the yogini becomes completely absorbed in Shiva, who is invoked here as *Shĕnkar* or Shankara.

Poem 50 caroms off the closing images of poem 49, with Lalla recounting, in her vigorous way, how she pestled her heart in love's mortar, then roasted and ate it: overflowing love for the Divine actually achieves a productive restraint over passion, and yet Lalla is assailed by momentary doubt. After this sacrifice of the self at the altar of the Self, will the questor live or die: meaning, will her life continue as before or will it be radically transformed?

51. G: 82 | K: 94

ōṁ-kār yĕli layĕ onum

Poem 51 opens with an account of a Yogic exercise, clearly including an element of *pratyāhāra*, the stopping-up of sensory inputs and the repetition of the primal syllable Om, until the rhythms of the body's vital breaths have been harmonised at a pitch of radiant intensity. The six roads in poem 51 refer to the six *chakras*, previously visualised as six forests in poem 50, while the seventh road is the highest of the *chakras*, the nectar moon. The experience of arriving at the Field of Light, *prakāshĕ-sthān* in Kashmiri, is identical with that of uniting with Shiva described in poem 50: the transcendence of the self and the recognition of unity with the Self.

52. G: 4 | K: 98

damāh-dam korumas daman-hālē

This poem refers to two subtle, powerful Yogic breathing techniques known to practitioners as *ujjayi prāṇāyāma* and *bhastrikā prāṇāyāma*. In the first, the conventional pattern of breathing through the nasal passages is bypassed and the breath is directed, instead, through the throat, so as to exert a slight pressure on the carotid arteries, lower the blood pressure and stabilise the mental processes; in the second, which literally means 'bellows breath', the breath is charged until the practitioner speeds up her respiration to twice its normal rate, purifying the nervous system and clarifying the mental processes through oxygenation (Satyananda Saraswati 1983, 118–21). The blazing up of the lamp symbolises the awakening of the Self that results from the attentive pursuit of these practices, in conjunction with Lalla's ongoing quest, and which clears a path for her through the long night journey of the spirit.

53. G: 56 | K: 95

yē gŏrā Paramēshwarā!

54. G: 57 | K: 96

nābi-sthāna chĕy prakrĕth zalawāñī

Poems 53 and 54 are cast in the classic mode of Tantra, in which the female disciple asks the male teacher for clarification and receives wisdom; this archetypal situation mirrors the primal dialogic setting of Tantric teaching, when Shakti approaches Shiva for instruction. These poems refer to the rhythm of exhalations during the practice of *prāṇāyāma*, when Lalla notices that her shorter exhalations emerge cool while her longer exhalations emerge relatively hotter; such practices induce an extreme awareness of the micro-climates of the body's various organs and processes.

Her teacher's reply must be understood in terms of the inner body/spirit geography developed by the Yogic adepts: the main channel for subtle energy within the body is the *sushumna-nāḍi*, the base of which rests in an energy centre beneath the navel, sometimes called the sun, and whose uppermost extremity is the *sahasrāra* or nectar moon, situated in the brain region, which we have come upon several times already. During the practice of *prāṇāyāma*, the vital breath passes up and down this route in the form of currents. When the hot current rising from the sun beneath the navel passes through the throat by itself, it is longer and retains its heat; however, when it meets the cooler current descending from the nectar moon, it loses its heat and comes out shorter and cooler.

55. G: 35 | K: 104

samsāras āyĕs tapasiy

Having come into *samsāra*, the world of facades and trapdoors, the seeker has found her way out by means of what she calls *bōdha-prakāsh*, the light of the mind achieved in poem 52. For an illumined one, the distinctions between life and death, oneself and another, the extinction of one body and the emergence of another, are all dissolved. The logic of the dichotomy between *samsāra* and *mokṣa* has lost its grip on her consciousness.

56. G: 101 | K: 13

dēhacĕ larĕ dārĕ bar trŏpárim

This poem employs the pun on *prān*, onion/life-breath, which we have already encountered in poems 26 and 27. The onion-thief or thief of life is the worldly nature, which would rush out into the agora, eager for gossip, rumour and transaction; he must be trapped inside the body by the methods of *prāṇāyāma*, confined to the space of the heart that is both intimate and cosmic, sometimes poetically described by yogis as *hridaya-ākāśa*, the heart-sky, and be subjected to the discipline of the primal and formative mantra. This last part of the treatment of the wayward nature is pungently described by Lalla, using the language of corporal punishment: *ōmaki cōbaka tulumas bam*, 'I stripped him with the whip of Om.'

57. K: 24

gŏras pr'tsŏm sāsi latē

The figure of the guru is crucial to Lalla's poetry, and to the understanding of her spiritual journey. She invokes the guru variously as 'Māli' or 'Master' (poem 128), 'Siddha-Māli! Siddhŏ!' or 'Perfect Master! Perfected One!' (poem 35; translated here as 'Master, my Master'), and '*yē gŏrā Paramēśwarā*' or 'O Guru, Supreme Lord' (Poem 53; translated here as 'My Guru, Supreme Lord'). While some of Lalla's poems may well be inquiries or apostrophes addressed to her mentor, Siddha Śrīkāntha, the figure of the teacher or guide often serves as a proxy for, or manifestation of, the Divine in her poetry.

The *Kulārnava Tantra*, a central text of the Tantra system, is most illuminating on the subject of the identity between the teacher and the Divine in a Tantric teaching lineage:

> Śiva, the Omnipresent One, too exquisite to be perceived, the Ecstatic One, the Undivided, the Immortal, Like-unto-heaven, the Unborn, the Infinite—how is He to be worshipped? It is to answer this question that Śiva has assumed the body of a teacher and dispenses, if he is worshipped with passion, material [bhukti] and spiritual release [mukti]. Clothed in human form, Supreme Śiva Himself walks the earth, to the delight of all true disciples. (Arthur Avalon and Tārānātha Vidyāratna's 1916 translation, quoted in Zimmer 1984, 206–07)

The 'Nothingness' of which Lalla speaks here is the Void that is also Wholeness, the deep and unmanifest reality that is the ground state of the universe, and will be achieved after the yogi has emptied out all the contents, impressions and attachments of material existence from his consciousness: the *shūña* or Shunya of Hindu thought.

58. G: 17 | K: 66

dēv watā diworu watā

59. K: 65

laz kāsiy shīt nĕvariĕ

In poems 58 and 59, Lalla confronts the temple priest with pithy critiques of idol worship and animal sacrifice. Her mode of addressing the ritual specialist is direct and, in this context, almost insultingly familiar, coming as it does from a woman in a feudal society governed by patriarchal norms. In the third line of poem 58, for instance, she asks: 'Pūz kas karakh, hōṭa baṭā?' Dismissing the worship of an idol and the religious economy of the temple—'all stone'—she emphasises that the Divine is to be reached through the Yogic practice of prāṇāgnihōtra, the offering of the body's awakened vital energies.

In poem 59, she attacks the priest for offering a lamb or ram as sacrifice to the gods, contrasting the animal's modest and undemanding way of being, and the usefulness of its wool, to the cruelty, wastefulness and ingratitude involved in sacrificing it. While Hinduism has long been associated with non-violence and vegetarianism, animal sacrifice has traditionally been part of the worship of Shakti, the Great Mother, in the dynamic and even warlike forms of Durga and Kali. Goats are still killed as offerings at centres of Shakti worship such as the Kalighat temple in Kolkata and the Kamakhya temple in Kamrup, Assam.

Meat has traditionally been used as an offering in certain ritual elaborations of Kashmiri Hinduism. After the mass migration of Kashmiri Hindus from the Valley in the early 1990s, however, these distinctive practices have practically disappeared in their homeland. In a situation veined with multiple ironies, Kashmir's Hindu shrines are now staffed by priests from the Gangetic plains or elsewhere in the subcontinent, hired by the armed forces: these men enforce the vegetarian norms of mainstream Indian Hinduism strictly, and regard animal sacrifices with horror.

60. G: 65 | K: 111

Shiwa Shiwa karān hamsa-gath sŏrith

Shiva's name is the mantra that holds the potential of deliverance. The Swan's Way, no echo of Proust, is *hamsa-gath*, the mystical designation accorded to the famous utterance of realisation: '*sō-'ham*', 'I am He'. Recited as an *a-japa japa* or repetition that deepens from words into silence and awareness, the syllables of this utterance reverse and rearrange themselves as '*ham-sah*', which means swan. This graceful bird has therefore been used for many centuries, in India's wisdom traditions, to denote the illuminated questor. When used as a title or honorific, for yogis who are regarded as having achieved unity with the Shiva-principle indwelling within the individual consciousness, the word is expanded into '*Paramahamsa*' or 'Great Swan'.

The questor is seen to have achieved that state of being which the Bhagavad Gita refers to as '*nishkāma karma*' or action without thought of reward, and which the teacher J. Krishnamurti referred to as 'choiceless awareness'. Having passed beyond all dualities, he has focused his mind on transcendence, and goes through the motions of ordinary life like an actor in a play—with complete assurance and commitment, yet knowing that it is not identical with his real life.

The somewhat unusual and highly Sanskritic designation *sura-guru-nātha*, which I have rendered here as 'Teacher who is First among the Gods', translates literally as 'gods-teacher-lord' and refers to Shiva as Mahādeva, the Great God, and as Yogīsvara, the Lord of Yoga. This designation also appears in poem 109.

61. G: 45 | K: 67

kush pōsh tēl zal nā gatshē

I have clustered together, as poems 61–68, *vākhs* in which Lalla emphatically shifts the locus of religious life from ritual practice to spiritual practice: she contrasts the merely formulaic nature of inherited, outward observance against the transfiguring potentiality of firsthand, inner experience. In poem 61, Lalla dismisses the impedimenta of ritualism and points to the guidance of the guru and a deepening immersion in meditative states as far more reliable ways of achieving oneness with the Divine. As the seeker gains liberation from the causalities of everyday life and accumulates fewer and fewer residues of *karma* or action and reaction, the possibility of *mokṣa* or release from the cycle of rebirth grows ever more certain.

The spiritual teacher Eknath Easwaran explains the doctrine of *karma*, with eloquent brevity, in the Introduction to his translation of the Buddha's *Dhammapada*:

> What we think has consequences for the world around us, for it conditions how we act. All these consequences—for others, for the world, and for ourselves—are our personal responsibility. Sooner or later, because of the unity of life, they will come back to us. . . . *Karma* means something done, whether as cause or effect. Actions in harmony with dharma bring good karma and add to health and happiness. Selfish actions, at odds with the rest of life, bring unfavourable karma and pain. In this view, no divine agency is needed to punish or reward us; we punish and reward ourselves. This was not regarded as a tenet of

religion but as a law of nature, as universal as the law of gravity.... Unpaid karmic debts and unfulfilled desires do not vanish when the physical body dies. They are forces which remain in the universe, to quicken life again at the moment of conception when conditions are right for past karma to be fulfilled. (1987, 13–14)

62. G: 42 | K: 70

gagan tsay bhū-tal tsay

Since the Divine pervades all things, whether at the grand scale of the universe with all its elements or the intimate scale of the tray of offerings arranged for the *pūjā* or formal act of worship, what can the true devotee offer the Divine that It does not already contain?

63. G: 33 | K: 71

dwādashānta-mandal yĕs dēwas thajī

The Unstruck Sound is the *anāhata nāda*, the deep sound of the universe, the silence that lies beyond understanding and is serenity and perfection. The focused recitation of the primal syllable Om is traditionally thought to be a key to the Unstruck Sound. As practitioners know, the syllable Om is treated as a sequence of four sounds when recited, beginning with 'A', passing through 'U', gliding across the hummed 'M' and culminating in a threshold between sound and silence, which marks the fourth sound, the sound not produced by any event or stimulus, the sound of the Void: the *anāhata nāda*.

In Yogic practice, *anāhata* also refers to the fourth of the seven *chakras* or centres of psychic and life-breath energy within the body; it is believed to be located on the spine, directly behind the heart, and governs emotional life. This *chakra* is closely related to the seventh and highest *chakra*, the *sahasrāra* or nectar moon, whose physical site in the anterior fontanelle of the brain is denoted by Lalla as *dwādaśanta-mandal*, known in the Sanskrit technical literature of Yoga as the *brahma-randra*. This is regarded by practitioners as the place in the body where the Shiva-principle resides, which is why Lalla's yogi-protagonist knows 'the crown is the temple of Self'. Having achieved identity with the Divine, the questor can hardly worship himself: he has passed beyond the gestures of worship and supplication, and grasped the secret of the paradoxical-seeming Sanskrit mystical utterance, '*na devo devam archayet*' or 'None but a god may truly worship a god.'

64. G: 58 | K: 139

yih yih karm korum suh artsun

In the condition of *sahaja* or *sahaz*, Lalla asserts, the true devotee becomes permeated with the Shiva-principle. In that expanded state of being and consciousness, every gesture and word expresses the presence of the Divine.

65. G: 63 | K: 62

jñāna-mārg chĕy hāka-wörü

The image of the garden recurs several times in Lalla's poetry, as a space to be protected and nurtured, a site of discovery, transformation or ecstasy. In poem 68, she celebrates the soul's jasmine garden; in poem 69, she speaks of the heart's narcissus garden; in poem 83, she employs saffron gardens as her setting. The action of poem 65 takes place in a *hāka-wörü* or vegetable garden, such as is found even today in the Valley of Kashmir. Unusually, though, its cultivator has allowed goats to enter and graze. This garden of knowledge is the scene of a purification of the self from its accumulated karma: the vegetables are the residues of acts from previous lives that are carried forward into the present life; the goats are embodiments of those past acts.

When penned in by a hedge erected by weaving together spiritual and ethical disciplines, the goats of karma must confine themselves to feeding on what they find there. This is a metaphor for the practice of perfection of thought, feeling and effort that gradually eliminates all karma. The vegetables are eaten, the goats are killed, and the self gains the knowledge of liberation and is released from its karmic obligations. Reflecting the differences of style, stance and preoccupation within the LD corpus—the varying emphases of various contributors in different periods, in my view—poem 65, like poem 20, uses the metaphor of the animal sacrifice to articulate poetic and spiritual truths, in contrast to poem 59, which decries the ritual practice.

The term that Lalla uses to refer to the sacrificial animals is of special interest: *lāmā-chakra-poshu*, beasts bound for the circle of the mother goddesses. The Kashmiri *lāmā* is identical with the Sanskrit *mātrikā* or 'little mother', the personification of the female energies or *śaktis* of the principal divinities. Often worshipped in a group or circle of seven, known as the *sapta-mātrikās*, they were popular deities of fertility and abundance.

66. G: 39 | K: 68

kusu pushu ta kŏssa pushŏñī

67. G: 40 | K: 69

Man pushu tŏy yitsh pushŏñī

In these companion vākhs, structured as question and answer, we are taken into the heart of Lalla's spiritual practice, which transcends all ordinary ritual and performance. Poem 66 is spoken in the voice of a yaja-māna, the patron of a ritual ceremony, asking a series of questions about the preparations for such a ceremony, from the point of view of conventional worship. He fusses over its details and the standing of its officiants. Poem 67 responds in a manner that bypasses this level altogether, rephrasing the act of worship at a far more spiritually advanced plane. The garland-maker turns out to be the mind; his wife the desire for bliss; the flowers they will offer are those of adoration; the water of the holy aspersion is nectar from the sahasrāra; and the chant is the chant of silence, the a-japa japa, the 'sō-'ham' whose significance has been explained in the note to poem 60.

On the Tantric path, the seeker graduates through four stages of sophistication: the entry level involves the use of offerings, flowers and ritual diagrams, homa-pūjā; the next level involves the recitation of formulae of praise, japa-stuti; the third level is based on the mental retention of a chosen inner image, dhyāna-dhāranā; and the highest plane is that of sahaja-avasthā, or sahaz in Kashmiri, when the inborn divine nature has been fully realised and the seeker needs no props or aids to concentration. As the Kulārnava Tantra puts it: 'To-act-not [a-kriyā] is the highest form of worship [pūjā]; To-keep-silence [a-japa] is the highest recitation; Not-to-think is the highest meditation [*dhyāna*]; absence of desire is supreme fulfilment' (Arthur Avalon and Tārānātha Vidyāratna's 1916 translation, quoted in Zimmer 1984, 224–25).

68. G: 68 | K: 131

Lal bōh tsāyĕs sŏman-bāga-baras

Poem 68 is one of the most beautiful of Lalla's *vākhs*, as sensuously evocative as it is charged with an ecstatic devotionalism that does not surrender meekly to enlightenment but embraces it with wild passion. The word *sŏman* could mean, as in poem 6, one's own mind; or it could be read as the identically pronounced Persian word for jasmine. Following Grierson, I am delighted to retain both meanings in my rendering, so that the poem opens with Lalla entering her 'soul's jasmine garden', an image that conveys both visuality and fragrance. What she bears witness to, within herself, is the most exalted experience cherished by the Tantric philosophy, the overcoming of all binaries and the ascension into a state of transcendence: metaphorically embodied by Shiva and Shakti intertwined in sexual union. Overwhelmed by this vision, Lalla passes beyond living and dying, and throws herself into the lake of nectar, the reservoir of immortality, the *amrĕta-saras*.

This divine coupling, which is the most sacred symbolic image of Tantra, has arguably found exquisite iconic expression in the extraordinary *yab-yum* images of the esoteric Tantrayāna Buddhism of the eighth to the twelfth centuries, a religious system profoundly influenced by Śaivite Tantra. We think, at once, of the Bodhisattvas Mahāsukha, Vajradhara and Akṣobhya, represented in coition with their respective śaktis or Tārās. As Zimmer (1984, 201) writes:

> The Divine Essence, which is both Being, eternally at rest, and Motion, constantly at play, exists here, fixed in totally compelling, immobile form, beyond the oscillating shimmer of some time-bound gesture and beyond the transitoriness of the moment; it lives here in a pose of love, in the face of which all things bound to time and space—the onrushing, crashing breakers of desire and the prolonged drifting, gradual ebbing of bliss—are in our beclouded consciousness but fleeting reflections.

69. K. Pr: 56

dilakis bāgas dūrü kar gōsil

As S.S. Toshkhani has observed (see the note to poems 17 and 18 above), poem 69 is a quatrain composed or rephrased by a certain Azizullah Khan in the early nineteenth century. In consonance with my argument concerning the LD corpus as a multi-user domain built up by various, largely anonymous contributors over the centuries, I would prefer to retain the poem while indicating its provenance, with no attempt to source it back into the fourteenth century. Certainly, the office of the *tehsīldār* or tax-collector did not exist in the village economy of the historical Lalla's time. That said, the poem presents a moving portrait of the questor as patient gardener, pruning away the weeds of negative feeling from the heart, knowing that the narcissus of insight will blossom; meanwhile, Death awaits his moment, ready to press the accounts of karma upon the spirit that has barely shaken off the demands of the body.

70. G: 84 | K: 118

yih kyāh ösith yih kyuthu rang gōm
cang gōm tsaṭith hudahudañĕy dagay

71. G: 85

yih kyāh ösith yih kyuthu rang gōm
bĕrongu karith gōm laga kami shāṭhay

Companion vākhs, poems 70 and 71 open with an identical first line, which I have rendered as 'I can't believe this happened to me!' Grierson, reporting that the meaning of some of the key words appeared to have been lost over the passage of time, professes a surprising bafflement: 'These are two of Lalla's hard sayings which are unintelligible at the present day, although there is no dispute as to the text' (1920, 99). One of the words that troubled him in poem 70 is *hudahudañĕy*, in the second line; Professor Jayalal Kaul suggested that this was a reference to the hudhud or hoopoe. I find this suggestion both appealing and convincing, and have based my interpretation on it.

The hoopoe, distinguished by its brown crest and the long digger beak with which it taps at trees or the ground, is the mystical guide and leader of the group of birds who set out to meet the Simorgh, the King of Birds, in the Sufi master Farid ud-din Attar's beautiful allegorical poem, *Mantiq at-Tair* ('The Conference of the Birds', 1177 CE). Only thirty of the birds survive the arduous journey, and at its end, find only their reflections in a lake. They realise that they have themselves become the Simorgh, a Persian word that yields up the meaning of si-morgh, 'thirty birds':

> Their souls rose free of all they'd been before;
> The past and all its actions were no more.
> Their life came from that close, insistent sun
> And in its vivid rays they shone as one.
> There in the Simorgh's radiant face they saw
> Themselves, the Simorgh of the world—with awe
> They gazed, and dared at last to comprehend
> They were the Simorgh and the journey's end.

(ATTAR 1984, 219)

This Sufi allegory of the self's discovery of its unity with the Divine, while heterodox from a strictly Islamic point of view, is analogous to the Kashmir Śaivite approach, and may offer evidence of the confluences of ideas that took place along the Silk Route and its byways, which linked present-day China, Tibet, Kashmir, Afghanistan, Iran and Iraq, among other regions.

In poem 70, Lalla exclaims that a hoopoe has cut her claws off with his beak, which may indicate an experience of 'thunderclap enlightenment' induced by sudden insight or the poetics of shock, somewhat in the nature of a Zen *satori*. The truth of all her dreams strikes her in a sentence, but this enlightenment also creates a complex sense of being isolated and cut adrift in the cosmos, here symbolised by a lake. In poem 71, she seems to lament a topsy-turvy life, characterised by the mismanagement of choices, which she must set right by achieving fine-tuned insight into the true nature of the self.

72. G: 46 | K: 84

asi pŏndi zŏsi zāmi

As she does in poem 1, Lalla reminds the ascetic, who attempts to store up merit by visiting one shrine and pilgrimage centre after another, that the Divine is neither outside nor far away, but within. She administers this insight through a series of physical, viscerally intimate images: the Divine is not merely a *Doppelgänger* to the self, but laughs, sneezes, yawns and coughs for the self, as the self; and indeed, while performing all these clumsy variations on the practice of Yogic exhalation, is the self/Self. The slash between the two is eliminated when Lalla suggests the simple civility of recognition.

73. G: 9 | K: 85

bān golu tŏy prakāsh āv zūnē

The human body is a microcosm of the universe, in Yogic theory. Accordingly, as we have seen in the note to poem 54, the sun and moon mark the base and pinnacle, respectively, of the *sushumna-nāḍi*, the seven-*chakra* channel that is mapped onto the spine, and along which the body's psychic and life-breath energy must be aligned in Yogic practice. The sun, or *mūlādhāra chakra*, is situated in the abdominal region; and the moon, or *sahasrāra chakra*, in the brain region. In states of intense contemplative absorption, when the *chakras* have been fully activated and the *kuṇḍalinī* energy has been awakened, the awareness of the centres vanishes and only the faculty of thought remains. In yet deeper meditative states, from the Kashmir Śaiva point of view, thought with all its conceptual distinctions is also left behind, and all cognitive and affective powers are absorbed into the energy field of the Supreme. With consciousness itself re-absorbed into the Shiva-principle, the universe melts back into the Supreme, and the elements become emptied of their reality.

74. G: 11 | K: 89

tanthar gali töy manthar mŏtsě

75. G: 30 | K: 90

lūb mārun sahaz větsārun

76. G: 69 | K: 91

tsitta-turogu wagi hěth roṭum

Poems 74, 75 and 76 form a group of vākhs, sharing the same closing line: *shūñěs shūñāh mīlith gauv*, 'A void mingles with the Void.' To the Kashmir Śaivite, the world of appearances is not a counterfeit reality so much as it is the play or dream of the Divine, an expression of Shiva's desire to create form and motion as a counterpoint to formlessness and stillness: the aim of true knowledge is to understand how the universe extends from its Source, and is immersed back into it. The Void connotes, simultaneously, an absolute emptying-out of particularities as well as an unimaginable abundance of potentialities.

In poem 74, Lalla traces a trajectory of gradual re-absorption by which the world-as-manifestation is drawn back into the Supreme. The locus of knowledge shifts inexorably from the scribal to the oral to thought, and finally, to that space of recognition in which the Divine awakes from the dream of the universe and recognises its own transcendence. The same drama of awakening is phrased more directly as counsel in poem 75, and more lyrically in poem 76, where Lalla describes a Yogic experience of the expansion of being and consciousness through a threefold practice: the concentration of the mind, which is visualised as a high-spirited horse; a commitment to *prāṇāyāma*; and the activation of the *sahasrāra chakra*.

77. G: 26 | K: 52

tsitta-turogu gagani brama-wônu

Lalla visualises the mind as a powerful stallion capable of enormous feats of endurance, covering great distances at extraordinary speed, but cautions that it is capricious and dangerous too, and cannot be trusted without the bridle of wisdom to control it. Without that bridle, it could destroy the 'wheels of breath's chariot', by which she means *prāṇa* and *apāna*, the two principal life-breaths within the subtle body. In the Yogic system, the coordination of these life-breaths into a steady rhythm is an essential step towards preparing for the experience of enlightenment.

78. G: 14 | K: 122

Shiv guru tôy Kĕshĕv palānas

79. G: 15 | K: 123

Anāhath kha-swarüph shüñālay

Poem 78 poses an indirect question as a prophecy, which poem 79 answers or fulfils. The trinity of Shiva, Vishnu and Brahma are distributed within an equestrian metaphor that seems, at first glance, oddly festive. Shiva, here to be understood not as the Supreme but as a specific manifestation of the Supreme, the Re-maker of Worlds, is the horse, symbolising the route to enlightenment. Vishnu, as Preserver, is at the saddle, ready to take that route. Brahma, as demiurge Creator, is jubilant at the stirrup, eager to be off and away. But the ride will not commence until the yogi decides which god shall mount the horse.

Poem 79 articulates the yogi's apocalyptic vision of the Self rising within the self. Here we have Shiva as the Supreme Being, who strikes the deep sound of the universe (explained in the note to poem 63), whose body is space, whose home is the transcendental Void, who is not constrained by any conventional marker of identity. He is 'both Source and Sound', a reference to the Kashmir Śaiva model of the Supreme residing within an individual's subtle body, as a *bindu* or intense dot of light, surrounded by the coiled *parā-śakti*, or supreme energy. In the first stage of enlightenment, when immersed deep in meditation, the yogi receives a blessed vision of the *bindu* (in my rendition, Source). This, in turn, triggers off the *parā-śakti*, which awakens with a primal cry (in my rendition, Sound).

From the perspective of the history of technology, India did not possess the stirrup until it was introduced into the northwest during the first Turkic raids led by Altagin and Sabuktagin in the late tenth and early eleventh centuries, its use then diffusing gradually through the subcontinent.

80. G: 28 | K: 33

yĕwa türü tsali tim ambar hĕtā

81. G: 27 | K: 30

khĕth gaṇḍith shĕmi nā mānas

82. K: 27

khěna khěna karān kun no vātakh

In these three poems, with their vivid and compelling images, Lalla warns against the excesses of sensual gratification, the enslavement of the higher nature by the appetites. In poem 80, proposing a moderate way of life, she reduces the body to its essential mortality, envisioning it as merely 'pickings for jungle crows'. In poem 81, she paints Death and Desire as twin tempters, terrible behind their winning ways. And in poem 82, she satirises both the obsession with the pleasures of the table as well as the self-righteous cultivation of ascetic virtuosity, underlining the importance of balance.

83. G: 88 | K: 35

atha ma-bā trāwun khar-bā!

The ass that may ravage one's neighbours' saffron gardens, in poem 83, is the mind. It must be placed under the control of spiritual and ethical disciplines by the higher nature, Lalla teaches, before it gives in to whim or caprice and expresses itself in destructive, self-defeating ways. Since saffron is a prized, expensive commodity, the saffron gardens are sacrosanct precincts, and their violation could invite severe penalties. The poem ends with a suitably harsh image of responsibility for one's own karma. While many traditional societies, in Asia as in Europe, permitted men of standing to offer proxies to receive punishment on their behalf when sentenced, Lalla points out that the individual self cannot hope to pass on the karmic burden of its accumulated actions to a surrogate conscripted for the task.

The cadence of poem 83, as of poem 106, is calibrated to a taut, percussive music. In the original Kashmiri, poem 83 reads:

atha ma-bā trāwun khar-bā!
lūka-hünzü kŏng-wörü khĕyiy
tati kus-bā dāriy thar-bā!
yĕti nanis kartal pĕyiy

84. G: 71 | K: 37

Mārukh māra-būth kām krūd lūb

85. G: 43 | K: 36

yemi lūb manmath mad tsūr môrun

In these two closely related poems, Lalla exhorts the aspirant on the spiritual path to overcome the negative emotions that occupy the mind and eclipse the will to perfection. Poem 84 suggests a contemplative discipline that permits the aspirant to disarm such negative emotions by analysing them, releasing the energy they knot up, and emptying them of their psychic influence and karmic weight, so that they vanish like the phantoms they are. Poem 85 carries this logic further, showing that the elimination of all negative psychic contents eventually opens up a course leading to the True Lord or *sahaz Yīshwar* in Lalla's phrase. At the same time, the aspirant realises that the phenomenal world, manifested by the Supreme as a temporary reality, is predestined for negation and transcendence, 'made of ash'.

86. G: 23 | K: 41

manasqy mān bhawa-saras

Lalla's conception, in this poem, of the mind as the ocean of life is both poetically vibrant and philosophically rich. By the 'ocean of life', I would understand the experiences, memories, sensations, emotional investments, reflexes and propensities that an individual accumulates in the course of life; or, from the Indic perspective, many lives. In my view, Lalla inherits this conception from the philosophers of the Yogācāra school of Mahāyāna Buddhism (second to the fifth centuries CE), who first gave it powerful elaboration. It is no coincidence that Yogācāra was born and flourished in Gandhara and Kashmir, and has very clearly left its impress on later philosophical advances made by thinkers and practitioners in those regions.

The Yogācārins proposed the *citta-mātra* or 'mind-only' doctrine, widely misunderstood to represent a crudely solipsistic view that the world is merely the creation of mind. On the contrary, as the Buddhist scholar Andrew Skilton (1994, 123) observes, the Yogācārins argued

> not that everything is made of mind (as though the mind were some kind of universal matter), but that the totality of our experience is dependent on our mind. The proposition is that we can only know or experience things with our mind. Every sense experience is cognised by the mind, therefore the things that we know, every element of our cognition, is essentially part of a mental process.

Thus the Yogācārins developed a sophisticated psychology, positing the existence of the *ālaya-vijñāna* or storehouse consciousness, which underlay several other strata of consciousness, associated with the senses and the mind. The *ālaya-vijñāna*, which is present in every individual, plays a pivotal role in Yogācāra spiritual practice: the Yogācārin must contemplate the turbulent contents of this storehouse, confronting and reflecting upon them, fully grasping their influence on his conscious thoughts and actions, and gradually but surely eliminating them.

This practice is conveyed in Lalla's awareness that the mind as ocean of life—or, as we may say, the *ālaya-vijñāna*—can deliver up 'fire-harpoons that stick in the flesh', but which, when weighed, 'weigh nothing'. In the third line of poem 86, I meld two alternative readings of a key image, while leaving the sense of the utterance intact: *nārūcü chŏkh*, meaning 'wounds made by a fishing-spear'; or *nāratsi-chŏkh*, meaning 'wounds caused by fire'. The persistence of the Yogācāra model is also manifest in poem 65, where Lalla proposes the metaphor of the animals grazing in the vegetable garden, awaiting sacrifice.

87. G: 12 | K: 48

hĕth karith rājy phēri nā

Lalla begins with the portrait of an individual trapped in conflicting desires; with her empathetic insight into human nature, she notes that the desire for fame as a renouncer is as negative a mental state as the desire for dominance and control. Freedom from desire is the only route to immortality: she closes with lines in praise of the *jīvan-mukta*, the exemplar extolled by Abhinavagupta and other Kashmir Śaivite masters, one whose liberation from desire has emancipated him, even as he lives, from the cycle of rebirth. Like Shiva, he has passed beyond the binaries of subjective and objective, transcendent and immanent, pleasure and pain: he is simultaneously yogi and bhōgi, renouncer and enjoyer, and goes through life with a unique and luminous lightness.

88. G: 61 | K: 49

yuhu yih karm kara pĕtarun pānas

Lalla is inspired, here, by the Bhagavad Gita's key ethical teaching: that of 'nishkāma karma', action undertaken in the spirit of self-perfection and without thought of reward. With no hoard of anticipation, frustration, elation and restlessness to carry, the seeker performs his or her actions in a condition of spiritual elegance, of beatitude.

89. G: 70 | K: 53

tsĕth amara-pathi thŏvizi

As a wandering teacher, it is not improbable that Lalla had a small circle of disciples or that she taught transient acolytes. In this context, poem 89 may have served her as a teaching text—intended to guide the aspirant towards the practice of confronting the most disquieting and disruptive contents of the mind, which are usually the first to surface when one embarks on a course of silent meditation. The deliberate strategy of infantilising these monster thoughts would help neutralise them while the aspirant cultivates the meditative energy to gather his or her psychic resources into coherence.

90. K: 28

tsālun chu vuzmal ta traṭay

Most of Lalla's *vākhs* are autobiographical testaments of the questor's journey, with its agonies and its ecstasies; but she rarely permits herself to dwell on the personal sufferings she experienced before liberating herself from the world of householders and crossing over to the religious life. Poem 90 is perhaps one of the few utterances in the LD corpus that are personal in this sense, and it speaks of what she endured while making this transition: resilience is what she needed, and received as grace from the Divine, when she submitted herself willingly to the rigours of the quest. To 'stand in the path of lightning' is to yield yourself receptive to enlightenment and the sometimes violent and certainly irreversible transformation of consciousness it generates. To 'walk when darkness falls at noon' is surely a metaphor for the paradoxical and liminal experiences that many mystics report during their initiation. To 'grind yourself fine in the turning mill' is to refine yourself through deepening spiritual practice.

91. K: 42

rut ta krut soruy pazĕm

Lalla speaks here in the voice of equanimity, embodying the Bhagavad Gita's exemplar of the *stitha-prajña*: one who is unshakeably anchored in knowledge. This corresponds to the Buddhist ideal of *upekṣa* (Pali *upekkha*), which is one of the four *brahma-vihāras* or abodes of perfection—states of being-in-the-world and being-towards-the-world envisioned by the Buddha as immeasurable expansions of the self into an embrace with all sentient beings and the universe. The other three states are maitri/metta, loving-kindness; karuṇā, compassion; and muditā, the gift of feeling joy in the joy of others (Skilton 1994, 35).

When Lalla sings, 'I don't hear with my ears, I don't see with my eyes', she signals the suprasensory awareness that the yogi gains access to, through the sustained practice of pratyāhāra, mentioned earlier in the note to poem 51. As Swami Niranjanananda Saraswati of the Bihar School of Yoga explains: 'What do we do in this practice? First we become aware of the senses. Later on, we become aware of the thought process, and finally, we try to disconnect the senses and the thought process by observing them and eventually stopping their activity' (1995, 166). The 'jewel-lamp' or ratnadīp that 'burns bright even in a rampaging wind' is the Self awakened within the individual, the Shiva-principle that, once ignited, cannot be extinguished. This image is analogous to that of the precious jewel held within the lotus in Tantrayāna Buddhist usage: the Bodhi-citta or will-to-enlightenment in the body, the Buddha-principle in the cosmos, memorialised in the cherished Tibetan chant, Om maṇī padmē hum.

92. G: 21 | K: 38

gāl gáṇḍinĕm bōl párinĕm

93. G: 18 | K: 39

ōsā bōl párinĕm sāsā

94. G: 20 | K: 40

mūḍ zŏnith pashith ta kôru

'The adept of *Kulācāra* is a yogi, and once he reaches his goal of suprapolar existence, he becomes an irritation, a mockery, an enigma to a world continuing in differentiation and forms,' notes Heinrich Zimmer (1984, 219). Imagine how much worse the situation would be for a yogini. As a woman who had renounced society and walked away from an oppressive marriage, leaving behind the circumscribed role of wife, daughter and daughter-in-law, and adopting the life of the *parivrājikā*, the peripatetic spiritual seeker, Lalla attracted much derision. Many legends are current about the daily insults she faced.

In these three poems, Lalla answers her detractors. Her greatest protection is her self-assurance, her conviction that she has chosen the path best suited for her temperament and orientation. Accordingly, in poem 92, she declares herself immune to insults and curses; even if her detractors were to see the error of their ways and come to offer her 'soul-flowers', she smiles, this would mean nothing to her. A *stitha-prajña* and a *jīvan-mukta*, she remains indifferent equally to slander and to praise, to pleasure and to pain, for she is beyond them; as she says in poem 93, 'I belong to Shiva.' The realised soul is Shiva's mirror; the reference in the last two lines of the poem is to the highly polished metal mirrors of the fourteenth century, best cleaned with ashes.

And in poem 94, Lalla offers the aspirant a quick guide to survival, suggesting the strategy of maintaining an outward show of conformity, or even the deliberate cultivation of an eccentric or harmless personality. Such camouflage—which would assuage the suspicions or invite the scornful pity of the orthodox—gives the aspirant the necessary respite to conduct his or her spiritual experiments.

95. G: 94 | K: 21

gŏran wonunam kunuy watsun

Poem 95 is the *vākh* whose last line—in the original, 'taway *mě hyotum nangay natsun'*—has launched an infamous flotilla of writings about Lalla's supposed espousal of nudity. These range from the sensational portraits of 'Kashmir's naked saint' put about by well-meaning New Agers, to the equally solemn ripostes of outraged commentators who claim purely metaphorical significance for the nakedness that Lalla celebrates here, and explain away the reference to dancing as merely a synonym for 'being' or 'walking'. For one party, Lalla is the wild woman who defies the most basic norms of a patriarchal society; for the other, she is the chaste Brahmin woman, apparently mindful of the sensitivities of future generations even while she goes about demolishing various canonical strictures.

Both parties in this contention overlook that Lalla elsewhere mentions her skirt (poem 45) and a robe (poem 146), indicating reasonable acquaintance with other sartorial choices. On a more serious note, the poem is centred on the mandate of inwardness: at the heart of inwardness, for the yogi or yogini, is Shiva. As Alain Danielou observes, 'All the teachings of yoga and the process of liberation are witnessed by the yogi in the cavern of his heart as the form of Maheśvara' (1991, 202).

To become identical with Shiva is to become indifferent to one's outward form, one's skin and clothes; significantly, one of Shiva's iconographical attributes is that he is *dig-ambara*, sky-clad, naked. Poem 95 thus yields up several levels of meaning. It could be read to mean that, in her ecstatic state of communion with the Divine, Lalla has cast away the construct of her identity

as an individual separate from the Supreme, as exemplified by
her clothes. It could also be read to mean that the yogini who
has realised Shiva has no need of the costume of social sanction
or conditional protection: she is liberated from the codes of
patriarchal authority that determine and constrain her social
behaviour. In this, Lalla's stance is analogous to that of the
twelfth-century Vīraśaiva woman saint-poet from Karnataka,
Mahādēviyakka, who cast off her clothes and went about mantled
only by her tresses (see Ramanujan 1973, 112).

96. G: 62 | K: 22

rājěs bŏji yěmi kartal tyŏji

Lalla sets up an array of desires here, with the necessary
prerequisites that correspond to them. She begins with political
power, which can be secured by military force, and goes on
to religious merit, which can be acquired through penance
and the performance of conventional good works. But true
enlightenment, Lalla argues, can result only from the instruction
of the guru, who directs the seeker towards knowledge of his
or her karmic profile, and indeed of the Self.

97. G: 72 | K: 29

tsala-tsitta! wŏndas bhayě mŏ bar

In an intriguing reversal of the usual division of attributes,
Lalla credits the mind, usually the stable seat of reason, with
prompting restlessness and fear in the heart, usually the mercurial
centre of emotion. In the oblique rhetoric of poem 97, the true
addressee is not the mind but the Divine, who is reminded of

the self's hunger for transcendence, its need to be carried across the ocean of life.

98. G: 51 | K: 77

zanañĕ zāyāy ráti tŏy kátiy

99. G: 52 | K: 78

yŏsay shĕl pīṭhis ta paṭas

100. G: 53 | K: 79

rav mata thali-thali tŏpitan

101. G: 54 | K: 81

yihay matru-rūpi pay diyē

102. G: 80

zānahŏ nāḍi-dal mana raṭith

Poems 98, 99, 100, 101 and 102 form a group of vākhs, linked by their closing line: *Shiv chuy krūṭhu ta tsēn wŏpadēsh*, here translated as 'But Shiva can play hard to get: hold on to that message.' In each of these five poems, Lalla invites the listener or reader to attend to a brief exposition of this theme. Each poem serves as a caveat, it would appear, to the aspirant who imagines that the quest will inevitably culminate in enlightenment, oblivious to the misadventures, errors, failures and disappointments that lurk along the route.

Poem 98 dwells on the arduousness of the journey towards enlightenment, the series of births over which it is staged; the beauty of the newborn is contrasted with the patience required to wait at the door of transcendence, the compression of the poem leaving it to us to imagine the hopes, anxieties, dreams and frustrations of the years between the two events, recurring over many lives. Poem 99 is crafted around the ubiquity of stone and the diverse material and symbolic valencies it can bear: in the walls of the temple, as flagstones on the road, as the basis of earth and territory, as the grinder in the mill. Similarly, Shiva too is everywhere and appears in diverse manifestations, but cannot be grasped without a deep commitment to the contemplative life.

In poem 100, Lalla speaks of the impartial manner in which the sun and water make no distinction between one country and another, one house and another; but Shiva, she implies, does make distinctions. At first glance, this may seem surprising, since Shiva is universal, suprapolar and beyond all binaries. The esoteric meaning of the *vākh* is that knowledge of the *sahaja* or *sahaz*, while theoretically available to all who seek it as the ground nature of their being, can only be attained by those who apprentice themselves to the wisdom traditions, who apply themselves to mastering the techniques of breath control and right mindfulness.

Poem 101 sits oddly in the mouth of a woman mystic and poet, since it rehearses a schedule of prescribed roles for a woman as mother, wife and temptress, collectively representing a life cycle in the course of which the self is nurtured, flourishes, and dies. If the aspirant thinks that the same inevitability attends the quest, he or she is mistaken: Shiva is not, if we go along with the rhetoric of this poem, so alien to our post-feminist sensibilities, as predictable as woman. Given the unpredictability of her own choices, it seems bizarre that Lalla would deploy such an analogy; on this count alone, I would speculate that this poem was added to the LD corpus at some point by an anonymous male contributor.

Lalla uses a mixed allegory in poem 102. She passes rapidly from expressing the wish to improve her command over *prāṇāyāma* by cutting and binding her breath-streams or *nāḍis*, which would allow her to refine the flow of her vital life-breaths, to wishing she could have crushed pain—all as prelude to fulfilling the alchemist's dream, discovering the Elixir of Life, which is a symbol for the knowledge of the Self here.

Poem 102 draws on the resources of breath control, surgery and alchemy, all three regarded as the most refined sciences of Lalla's time and place, with lineages going back a millennium into the past. These sciences had been codified by thinkers who enjoyed the patronage of the Kushan rulers. The Kushan empire, which endured from the first to the fourth centuries CE, marks a most unfortunately undervalued period in Indian history. Among its capitals and prominent regions were Purushāpāra (present-day Peshawar, in Pakistan), Oddiyāna (once a centre of Buddhist learning, today the vexed and Taliban-brutalised Swat Valley, in Pakistan), and Śrīnagara (today's Srinagar, Kashmir).

It was under the Kushans—originally West Central Asian immigrants who choreographed a confluence of Indian, Greek, Chinese and Persian cultural energies—that epochal advances were made across a range of fields and disciplines. To list only a few of these: the Buddha was bodied forth as a human image for the first time, as well as given a biography by Aśvaghosa; Mahāyāna Buddhism emerged as a distinct system under the patronage of the Kushan ruler Kanishka; the deities that we now regard as definitively Hindu were rendered into iconography for the first time, including Shiva, Vishnu and Shakti; indeed, Shakti was first introduced into India, as a naturalised version of the West Asian war goddess Nanaia; and medicine and surgery made the transition from oral archives to sophisticated written treatises, in the hands of masters like Charaka and Jīvaka. All these developments flow into the time horizon of Lal Dĕd and have a significant bearing on her own work as well as that of her contemporaries. As we have seen, Mahāyāna Buddhist philosophy and the presence of the Mother Goddess through the medium of Tantra underpin Lalla's ideas, images and allegories in crucial ways.

103. G: 16 | K: 83

tūri salil khoṭu tŏy tūrē

As the action of the sun on ice and snow reveals, water, in all its avatars, remains essentially water. Lalla employs this metaphor to expound a central teaching of Kashmir Śaiva philosophy. In this account, all things are manifestations of the Supreme Consciousness: they are created in the playful spirit of *spanda*, the originary vibration by which the Supreme Consciousness extends Itself into the universe; when the outward phase of the vibration returns to its source, the differentiated forms of the universe dissolve back into unity.

104. K: 57

Shiv chuy thali-thali rōzān

Often and widely cited as evidence of Lalla's indifference to sectarian distinctions and her embrace of Hinduism as well as Islam, poem 104 is a manifestly late addition to the LD corpus or a comparatively recent recasting of earlier material. It does not appear in the Darwĕsh–Śāstrī–Grierson line of transmission, but was included by Professor Jayalal Kaul in his meticulously framed and authoritative Lal Dĕd collection, although Kaul insisted that no categorical assurances could be offered as to the 'authenticity' of much extant LD material.

The second line of this poem, mō zān hyŏnd ta musalmān, uses the designations 'Hindu' and 'Muslim', which were not current during the historical Lalla's lifetime. During that period, Hindus were more likely to be known by their caste membership, and Muslims were known throughout the subcontinent as 'Tūrka' or 'Tūrushka', denoting Turki or Turkic, the ethnicity to which many Muslims who settled in India between the eleventh and fourteenth centuries belonged. And while the Arabic title of sāhib or 'Lord', applied to Shiva in the last line of this poem, offers pleasing evidence of a cross-fertilisation between languages, it does not necessarily mark a synthesis of religious ideas.

While the Śaivite questor takes, as his mandate, the establishment of the seamless identity between seeker and Sought, it would be blasphemous for the Muslim questor to imagine that the human individual and the Divine could, at any level, be of the same essence. The Sufis courted the anger of the orthodox for their suggestions in this latter direction; indeed, the Persian mystic Mansūr al-Hallāj (c. 858–922) was executed by the Abbasid Caliphate for daring to declare, 'Anā l-Haqq', translatable either as 'I am the Truth' or 'I am God', utterances that form the basis of Vedantic spiritual practice.

That said, the ecumenical sentiment of poem 104 resonates

with the Kashmir Śaivite conviction that the differences between self and other, appearance and reality, are illusory, since all dualities are pervaded and supervened by the Shiva-principle. It should also be remarked that the originally Arabic title of *sāhib* has been adopted organically into the ceremonial language of syncretic traditions in India that have drawn both on Hinduism and Islam, such as the Nanak-*panth*, universally known as Sikhism, founded by Guru Nānak Dēv (1469–1539) and codified by the nine Gurus who succeeded him. The Sikhs had already spread widely across the subcontinent by the seventeenth century, settling in the Valley of Kashmir as well. It is not improbable that the language of poem 104 could reflect the anonymous LD contributor's acquaintance with Sikh usage. The chief scripture or 'Primordial Book' of Sikhism, for instance, is described as the *Guru Granth Sāhib*; this honorific is also applied to the major Sikh shrines, such as *Harmandir Sāhib* and *Śīsganj Sāhib*.

105. K: 82

Shiv chuy zävyul zäl vaharävith

In consonance with the theory of *spanda*, mentioned in the note to poem 103, the Divine is seen here as a recovery net that spreads out to trap and trawl back all the manifestations of Itself. Not only does the Divine pervade the universe but It also permeates the individual self. This vision of wholeness and re-integration waits to disclose itself to the prepared consciousness. Prepare your consciousness to receive it in this life, says Lalla, because it is in the present that such a vision matters the most. Now is your best chance to transfigure the course of your life. There is no exalted vision of the Divine in the afterlife, for the Kashmir Śaivite—since the afterlife, for the unprepared or half-baked consciousness, is merely the next birth, a return to the fate of standing and waiting for the door of transcendence to open, as poem 98 puts it.

106. G: 87 | K: 17

niyĕm karyŏth garbā

This poem shares the same cadence as poem 83, a song-like beat that quickens our perception of its teaching: the self comes into the world with a mission from a previous birth, that of continuing the quest for transcendence; but the memory of this mission weakens and is overwritten by fresh experiences and new memories, the resolve made in the previous life vanishes, and only a stern rebuke from a teacher such as Lalla herself can recall the migrant self to its resolve. To die to the traffic of desire, dream and sorrow while yet alive, to arrive at the serene state of the jīvan-mukta, is the ideal to which the seeker launched on the path of Kashmir Śaivism aspires.

107. K: 54

kus mari tay kasū māran

108. K: 55

gŏr śabdas yus yatsh patsh barē

The sentence of execution that preoccupies these companion poems refers, not to a physical death, but to the possibility of spiritual suicide. Lalla makes reference here, clearly, to the backslider who gives up at an early stage of the journey towards enlightenment and lapses again into worldly affairs, and the intellectual, emotional and moral variability that these demand.

In poem 107, having given up the incremental meditation on Shiva's name ('*hara hara*' or 'Shiva! Shiva!'), the backslider runs around the circuit of home and work, profit and advancement ('*gara gara*' or 'My house! My house!'). He thus loses the opportunity for self-overcoming, and condemns himself to a new lease of servitude to the cycle of rebirth. In poem 108, Lalla has better news for the backslider, a conditional 'come back, all is forgiven': trust the guru, practise the perfection of mindfulness, gain mastery over the senses, she says, and you earn your reprieve from the cycle.

109. G: 5 | K: 133

par tŏy pān yĕmi somu mônu

The fully realised exponent of Kashmir Śaiva philosophy has received the vision of Shiva, described here, as in poem 60, as *sura-guru-nātha*, the 'Teacher who is First among the Gods'. He has savoured the omnipresence and omnipotence of the Shiva-principle, and understood that the transcendent and the immanent, the unchanging and the mutable, are expressions of the same Supreme Being. At the social level, accordingly, such an enlightened self also renounces the distinctions between self and other.

110. K: 103

shūñuk mā' dān kōdum pānas

Lalla's solitary traversal of the Field of Emptiness, an experience of the Void in its infinite vacancy of manifestation yet plenitude

214

of possibility, evidently comes about after a deep immersion in the practice of *pratyāhāra*, when the senses are withdrawn from their sense-objects, the reason is gradually superseded and a range of suprasensory experiences open up. This has already been spoken of in the notes to poems 51 and 91. The experience of the Field of Emptiness is identical with that of Lalla's arriving at the Field of Light in poem 51. The transcendence of self and the recognition of its identity with Shiva is the secret that belongs to the questor, as to every individual, in Kashmir Śaiva theory; yet few even know that they possess a secret of such magnitude. The awakened consciousness—purified of karmic residues and luminously replete in its unity with the Supreme—is the lotus that rises from the marsh of existence, sensory attachments, and the confusions and mixed motives of an unexamined life. The lotus rising from a marsh could also be a deeply moving self-portrait: Lalla as she saw herself, retaining the purity of her vision in an unpromising social environment.

111. K: 47

parum pōlum apŏruy purum

Lalla takes a pragmatic view of learning. Having imbibed all that the scriptures and treatises of Kashmir Śaivism and Yoga had to teach her, she experimented beyond them, a prepared questor apprenticing herself to direct experience. As a result of this, she is no mere scriptural expert or ritual specialist, but an adept, a living master. There is no divergence between what she teaches and what she practices. Always ready to grapple robustly with life and its challenges, Lalla has entered the forest of the spirit, where the seeker must confront her or his deepest terrors and phantoms, and emerged victorious. She has 'wrestled with the lion', which here symbolises worldly ambition, stripping it of its power to dominate the individual's imagination and monopolise her or his energies.

112. K: 127

tan man ga'yas bŏh kunuy

113. K: 132

chuy dīvu gartas tu dartī srizakh

Poems 112 and 113 are songs of praise for the Divine. Yet, even in a hymn of surrender such as poem 112, when Lalla describes the experience of the clear note of the Divine ringing through her, she retains the freedom of agency: her being and consciousness amplified far beyond the horizons of normality, she situates herself in the totality of the expanded universe, figuratively gaining access to the celestial as well as the infernal regions. In poem 113, Lalla invokes the Divine as Transcendence: as the ruler of the universe; as the inspiration behind the five great elements that sustain the world; as the *anāhata nāda*, the deep sound of the universe, which is the silence that opens at the edge of sacred words; and as infinite extension, beyond the reach of ordinary instruments of measurement.

114. G: 1 | K: 134

abhyōsi savikās layĕ wŏthū

115. G: 2 | K: 135

wākh mānas kŏl-akŏl nā atē

216

116. G: 59 | K: 136

tsah nā bŏh nā dhyēy nā dhyān

117. G: 93 | K: 138

tsĕth nowuy tsạndarama nowuy

In the four poems that I have grouped together as 114–17, Lalla describes and celebrates the state of transcendent awareness, achieved through intense Yogic practice, when the known and perceptible universe reveals itself as a subsidiary manifestation of the Supreme. In this state, all normal faculties are transcended, along with their lexicon of names and forms, mind-focusing devices and metaphysical concepts.

Poem 114 turns on its second line: *gaganas sagun myūlu sami tsraṭā*. Literally, this can be rendered as 'The manifest and qualified universe merged completely with the sky (or Ether, or the Infinite).' I have chosen to focus on the nuance of the seemingly simple onomatopoeic word, *tsraṭā*, which conveys the sound of water splashing on water, to demonstrate the recognition of complete identity between the manifest universe and the Infinite, leading the seeker to the awareness of the Void. In Kashmir Śaiva thought, however, this recognition does not constitute final enlightenment, but is a threshold leading to complete absorption in the Supreme. The Void is an intermediate phase in the process by which the Supreme associates Itself with Māyā, or cosmic illusion, to manifest Itself in the particularities that we know as the world we experience. By passing beyond the Void, in the final stage of Yogic absorption, the seeker reaches awareness of the Supreme, which Lalla describes as *anāmay*, purified of all illusion, illimitable consciousness.

217

In poem 115, Lalla makes plain that the state of transcendent awareness is beyond the domain of the discursive and the conceptual: it cannot be captured in words or mapped in thoughts. My rendering, 'normal or Absolute', represents Lalla's kŏl-akŏl. The word kŏl means 'family' (from the Sanskrit kula), and refers to the constellation of the jīva or individual soul, prakṛti or primal matter, space and time, and the five elements of earth, water, fire, air and ether. These form the basis of normality; that which transcends these is akŏl, the Absolute. Taken together, the normal and the Absolute embody all creation, both the manifest and the Unmanifest. All this is left behind by the yogi in the state of transcendent awareness. Even Shiva and Shakti are seen to be constructs, provisional conceptions that are not identical with the Supreme, but only symbols and indications of it. The Supreme is the Unnameable, the grand surplus that exhausts all our attempts at naming and form-making, decipherment and approximation, in Lalla's teaching.

In poems 114 and 115, as elsewhere in the LD corpus, it is the scholar-priest, tied to his routines of prayer, scriptural citation and observance, who receives the brunt of Lalla's thunderclap counsel.

Lalla continues to contour the state of transcendent awareness in poem 116. She indicates the blurring of the sharp lines separating personal identities and their interests, and also the dissolution of the separation between the object of contemplation and the act of contemplation itself. What the seeker now realises is that the world is the Supreme as associated with Māyā, 'the All-Creator, lost in His dreams'. Some remain at this level of understanding of the Void, but others plunge deeper into enlightenment, and become fully absorbed into an understanding of Perfection.

The infinitive *layun* plays a crucial role in poems 114 and 116. It means both the attainment of beatitude and a dissolution into the cosmos, Nothingness or Perfection. Here, as in Indic metaphysics and Indian classical music, the word, with its noun form *laya*, carries the sense of a deeply resonant and unceasing rhythm: a structuring and patterning of time and experience into combinations of movement and pause; a wave of creation and dissolution from which notes and motifs arise, and into which they drown only to be re-made. Seemingly outside oneself, *laya* is suddenly recognised as resonating inside oneself and, in some sense, having always resided and resonated inside oneself.

The sense of *laya* is carried forward in poem 117, which is a celebratory hymn charged with the presence of *pralaya* (*zalamay* in Kashmiri), the deluge that enacts a cosmic dissolution at the end of every *kalpa* or cycle of time and marks the beginning of the next, in Indic cosmology. Lalla delights in a vision of regeneration, the world enchanted once again, suffering and delusion cleansed away: the mind, freed of its phantoms, is new; the moon, whether as activated *sahasrāra*, earth's satellite or ornament in Shiva's hair, is new. Lalla, evidently recounting the experience of many past lives and periods, has seen the cosmic ocean renewed epoch after epoch. These epic-scale regenerations are reflected in Lalla's own transfiguration, through the rigorous self-purification of Yogic practice.

118. G: 24 | K: 64

shīl ta mān chuy pôñu kranjě

119. G: 38 | K: 113

zal thamawun hutawah taranāwun

219

120. K: 63

shishiras vuth kus raṭe

121. G: 34 | K: 72

okuy ōṁ-kār yĕs nābi darē

In the four poems sequenced here as 118–21, Lalla develops a portrait of the true yogi or yogini. She meditates on sham and substance, contrasting the easily acquired reputation of the showman with the genuine worth of the contemplative. In poem 118, she lays out a series of impossible conditions—reputation is water in a fisherwoman's leaky basket—and asks around for someone who can perform superhuman feats not met with outside fantasy literature, as a possible candidate for belief in the *vanitas* of reputation.

In poem 119, Lalla dismisses the miracle-mongering of self-styled spiritual adepts who remain trapped at the level of demonstrating their *vibhūtis* or *siddhis*—the paraphysical powers that the yogi or yogini acquires as incidental effects during the process of attaining *prajñālōka*, the light of perfect knowledge—in order to attract and hold the attention of the swelling ranks of their devotees. Lalla disposes of such performances summarily, as *sakolu kapaṭa-tsarith*, blatant charlatanry.

When poem 120 begins, we suspect that Lalla is about to launch another denunciation of mountebanks parading as saints, but her tropes of impossibility are not satirically intended or purely rhetorical this time. She proposes the yogi, one who has conquered his senses, as one who can also command the elements, the seasons and the cycle of day and night, metaphorically indicating his anchorage in the Self and his consequent indifference to all rhythms of change. Poem 121 offers a portrait of the realised yogi, whose breath, contained and amplified within his body through the discipline of *kumbhaka* or the 'jar exercise', prepares him for the demanding act of focusing, body and soul, on the Supreme. A yogi at this stage of accomplishment no longer chants consciously: his chanting of the supremely powerful mystic syllable Om has achieved constancy, and emanates from the centre of the body's life-force, which is known in Yoga as the *kanda* or bulb and is situated beneath the navel. Since he is animated by the puissance of Om, the mantra of mantras, he has no need for any other incantations.

122. G: 55 | K: 109

kandĕv gēh tĕzi kandĕv wan-wās

123. G: 64 | K: 110

kalan kāla-zōli yidaway tsĕ golu

124. G: 32 | K: 112

kĕh chiy nĕndri-hátiy wudiy

125. G: 6 | K: 119

tsidānandas jñāna-prakāshĕs

In the four *vākhs* arranged here as poems 122–25, Lalla addresses herself to the classic question of choice that many aspirants must make: Should they take up their responsibilities in the world of householders, or should they renounce society and retreat to the forest, the hermitage, the monastery? Lalla suggests that we should attend, not to one option over the other, but to the cultivation of mindfulness and steadfast dedication of purpose in whatever path we choose to take through life. In poem 122, she notes that the restless individual could escape from home or from the hermitage, since it is not the external situation but the inner temperament that prompts such impulsive, erratic action: 'No orchard bears fruit for the barren mind.' Similarly, in poem 123, she makes no distinction between hermit and householder. You are as good as the accuracy and intensity of your knowledge: what matters is whether you have 'dissolved your desires in the river of time'. If you have, you will be graced with transcendent awareness, the vision of the Self as perfection.

A formal choice is no guarantee of the fulfilment of the wish implicit in that choice, as Lalla demonstrates in poem 124, and yet redemption lurks in the most unlikely circumstances. There are those who can be fully aware even in their sleep, there are those who sleepwalk open-eyed through life, captives of illusion and delusion. Then there are those who cannot wash their sins away even by bathing in holy ponds; and those who lead busy lives in the world of affairs and anxieties, yet their souls remain untouched and radiantly clear. This last class of people are the jīvan-muktas, and Lalla praises them in the first two lines of poem 125: 'Those who glow with the light of the Self / are freed from life even while they live.' As the Kulārnava Tantra expounds:

The yogi enjoys sensual pleasures in order to help mankind, not out of desire; he is at play upon the earth, delighting all men, [that is how he conceals his true nature]. . . . the yogi is all-scorching like the sun, all-consuming like the fire; he enjoys all pleasures and yet he

remains without blot or blemish. He touches everything
as does the wind; he permeates all things as does the air.
(quoted in Zimmer 1984, 219)

In sharp contrast to the realised ones, however, are the fools—
who continue to burden themselves with ill-considered actions
and their karmic residues, trapping themselves ever more
securely in the 'tangled net of the world'. The metaphor of the
world as a jāla or net, in which all beings are caught, is one that
recurs in the poems, songs and teaching stories of India's wisdom
traditions. Likewise, the figure of the fool appears repeatedly in
the same texts, as a cautionary tale about the necessary limits
that a healing wisdom must set for itself.

We could speculate that these poems were answers originally
given by Lalla—possibly as improvised, spontaneous replies that
were later shaped into scribal form—to questioners who came
to her for advice on the shape and direction of their lives.

126. K: 18

muḍās gyānac kath nō vanizē

127. K: 19

dachinis ŏbras zāyun zānaha

In poems 126 and 127, as in poems 40 and 41, Lalla warns
against the error of throwing wisdom away on one unprepared
to receive it. Her metaphors are drawn from everyday life:
sugar for an ass, which has no taste for it; the shifting sands of
the riverbank or the riverbed; oil poured on cattle fodder; the
southwest monsoon; and the patience of the physician.

128. K: 45

avĕtsāri pothĕn chihō māli parān

Lalla dismisses the practice of chanting from the scriptures by rote, with no understanding of the emancipatory potential of the words of wisdom and power contained in these texts. Here, as in poem 111, Lalla's approach to enlightenment is an experimental, experiential one. Bypassing the scriptures, she regards the transmission of redemptive wisdom as taking place through the medium of discipleship: she underscores the importance of a guru's direct teaching, presence and grace, and indicates that the true teaching passes from master to disciple as a direct, often unspoken but unmistakeably made gift. The 'greatest scripture', she insists, is beyond words and beyond sound. Her approach is remarkably congruent with those of the Siddha masters of late Tantrayāna Buddhism and the exponents of the *dhyāna* or Zen schools.

129. K: 46

parun sôlab pālun dôrlab

In the same spirit as the preceding poem, this *vākh* points up the contrast between the scholar's life, devoted to the study of texts, and that of the active seeker, whose text is the totality of experience. Practice is viewed, with some self-irony on Lalla's part, as a fog, which, instead of blinding the unwary traveller caught in it, clears an occasion for profound insight.

130. G: 47 | K: 114

yĕth saras sàri-pholu nā vĕtsiy

This poem is structured around a wonderful play of scale that connects the infinitesimal to the cosmic. In comparison with the Infinite, Lalla says, the world is a lake so small that not even a mustard seed could sink in it. And yet this seemingly insignificant lake is the vast reservoir where all beings come, metaphorically, to drink water; where all beings are born and die, and are born again. Among the beings listed in poem 130, I have translated *zala-hâstiy*, literally 'water-elephants', as 'cloud-elephants', since this is what the word seemed to imply: a personification of the pluvial aspect of the water cycle.

The symbolism of the mustard seed occurs both in the Buddhist and the Christian wisdom traditions. The Buddha, in a parable concerning the inevitability of death, asks a grieving woman who wants him to revive her dead child, to bring him a mustard seed from a family in which no one has ever died; naturally, she cannot. She gains an insight into the nature of desire, sorrow, change and wisdom; and the mustard seed became a symbol for right understanding (see Easwaran 1987, 41–42). Jesus, in a parable concerning the nature of the Kingdom of Heaven, compares it to a mustard seed—which, though the smallest of seeds, once planted, grows into a large tree with many branches, and offers shelter to many birds (Luke 13: 18–19; Mark 4: 30–32; Matthew 13: 31–32).

Such symbolisms were in active circulation, for nearly a millennium between the first and seventh centuries CE, along the Silk Route that linked the deep heart of Western China with the Eastern Mediterranean, and included Kashmir in its larger ambit. Buddhist, Hindu, Zoroastrian, Manichean and Christian ideas, practices and iconographies are known to have been transmitted along the cities of the Silk Route and diffused further, through the interactions of monks, merchants, scholars, storytellers and translators. Among the many examples of this flourishing cultural confluence is the fact that a number of stories from the Buddhist Jatakas eventually found an afterlife as tales about Jesus or various Christian saints, through the writings of St John of Damascus; similarly, a number of stories from the *Panchatantra*, the *Hitopadeśa* and the Ramayana found their way into the narrative cycles of Boccaccio and Chaucer.

131. G: 50

trayi něngi sarāh sári saras

As in poem 117, Lalla offers an apocalyptic yet potentially redemptive vision of *pralaya*, the world-dissolving deluge. The world is again imagined as a lake: one that has overflowed its own shores three times, perhaps alluding to three cosmic cycles that Lalla has witnessed in previous lives. The 'lake mirrored in the sky', when nothing exists except water and sky, may refer to a *mahā-pralaya* or great deluge—when not only the known universe but also the realm of the gods and even the demiurge Creator, Brahma himself, are destroyed, to be replaced by a new Brahma, new gods, and a new world.

The reference to a lake bridging Mount Haramukh in the north with Lake Kausar in the south provides us with an ancient and mythic geography of Kashmir: the extent so described is, in fact, the Valley of Kashmir, which was said to have been a lake called Satī-saras at the beginning of our present *kalpa*. In the last line of this poem, Lalla claims to have seen the world vanishing into the Void seven times. These momentous acts of recall, these memories stretching across vast periods of time (a kalpa is reckoned by Hindu cosmologists as 432 million years) are intended to generate a sense of the incalculably long journey of the continually reborn self towards its ultimate release.

132. G: 81 | K: 116

mad pyuwum syundu-zalan yaitu

Lalla speaks here both as the individual self and as the voice of the Self, which has passed through many births on its voyage across the ocean of existence. The Sindhu is the Indus, one of Kashmir's principal rivers: its crystalline water is the wine that she has drunk over a concourse of births. The reference to eating human flesh seems to have puzzled or unsettled several observers. Following Grierson, I would annotate this image in the following way: Lalla visualises the Self here as an anthropophagic entity, one that has, metaphorically, consumed numerous bodies in passing through a sequence of lives. Admittedly this image is cast in the *rasas* or affective registers of *bhayānaka* (the terrifying) or *bibhatsa* (the disgusting), and so may not accord with the taste of readers who prefer their classical authors to be well-behaved, measured, circumspect and attentive to the proprieties. The truth is that Lalla is not a classical author in this limited sense; rather, she claims the authority of a classic by virtue of her thunder-loud utterances, her robust images and her lightning-clear insights, which pierce the heart of the universe.

133. K: 125

raṅgas manz chuy byŏn byŏn labun

Here, as in the preceding poem, Lalla employs the allegory of the world as a theatre: the venue for *līlā*, the play of forms by which the Unmanifest manifests Itself. The Self is the actor who has worn many personae on this stage, and vanishes behind the parts He plays. How can one find Him? By ridding oneself meticulously of all negative emotions, Lalla teaches, and by developing the qualities of equanimity and resilience.

134. K: 117

asi āsi tay asīy āsav

This poem revisits what I have called the 'dance of perpetual circularity', which Lalla dwells on in poem 8. The substance of the Self abides across time, even as the universe comes into being, is dissolved and is brought into being again. Shiva is invoked here as the Breaker of Worlds, as regular as the solar cycle, presiding over the wheel of existence, guiding every *kalpa* from one cosmic deluge to the next.

135. G: 78 | K: 120

kus ḍingi ta kus zāgi

136. G: 79 | K: 121

man ḍingi ta akŏl zāgi

Paired as question and answer, like poems 66 and 67, *vākhs* 135 and 136 carry the cadence of an initiation ritual. The questioner asks a series of questions of seemingly vast and cosmic-scale import, beginning with the memorable 'Who's asleep and who's awake?' The answers centre the locus of redemption in the bodied self: the mind and its ability to slough off the material attachments and parameters of space, time and particularity that weigh it down; the organs of sense, their energy replenished by the activated *sahasrāra*, are the lake from which a rain of nectar falls constantly; Shiva's favourite offering is 'knowledge of Self'; and the *parama-pad* or Supreme Word—this term can also mean 'Supreme Place'—that the seeker is looking for is *tsētana-Shiv*, 'Shiva-consciousness', the recognition that one is identical with the Shiva-principle. I have compressed this recognition as 'The Supreme Word you're looking for/is Shiva Yourself.'

137. K: 43

mandachi hānkal kar chaynām

As in poems 92–94, in which she responds to the curses and insults of her detractors, Lalla here contemplates the shame in which other people try and mantle her. She indicates the strategies by which the chain and robe of shame can be eliminated. Resilience is called for, as well as the need to curb and tame the wild horse of the mind, so that it remains focused on the inward quest and is not tempted to divert its energies into reacting to provocations.

138. K: 44

parān parān zěv tāl phajim

139. K: 34

treśi bŏchi mŏ kreśināvun

140. K: 31

kaṅdyo karakh kaṅdi kaṅdē

141. K: 32

sŏman gārun manz yath kaṅdē

In the small garland of poems from 138 to 141, Lalla
contemplates questions of spiritual hygiene, dwelling variously
on themes such as the relationship between the body and the
mind, the difference between the mere repetition of mantras and
the inspired entry into transcendent awareness, and the correct
attitude towards the body.

In poem 138, Lalla ridicules the mindless repetition of
prayers and chants, undertaken as quantitative performances meant
to generate spiritual merit rather than in the spirit of devotion
and self-overcoming. While they may exhaust the individual
physically—tongue cloven to the palate, thumb and finger raw from
telling the beads—they can neither qualify as true worship nor
can they purify the consciousness of its persisting discontents.

In vākh 139, Lalla turns the searchlight of critique on the
pursuit of mindless austerities. She addresses a perennial
tendency within haṭha-yoga—the branch of Yogic practice
dedicated to the purification of the body in preparation for
higher meditational exercises—which fetishises the cult of
self-mortification as an end in itself. Instead of brutalising the
body with fasts and extreme vows (which is really to yield to
the spiritual sin of arrogance), she urges the aspirant to practise

a rigorous morality: to demonstrate altruism and compassion, to release the self towards others and their needs. This poem, like poem 91, resonates with the Buddha's teaching of the *brahma-vihāras*, the accent here being specifically on *maitri/metta*, loving-kindness, and *karuṇā*, compassion.

Pointing to the inevitable fate of the body as a perishable vehicle for the Imperishable, in poem 140, Lalla deplores the obsession with the body as an expression of doomed and futile vanity. This poem has the ring of a meditation intended to guide the aspirant beyond normal, body-centred consciousness, and to pass beyond the illusion of the permanence of the body, its desires and idiosyncrasies. Such meditations on mortality are well documented in other spiritual traditions as well: for instance, the Aghora Śaivite practice of meditating in cemeteries, the Tantrayāna meditation on a skull, and the Catholic monastic exercise of contemplation in an ossuary.

In *vākh* 141, Lalla corrects the balance in favour of a sane respect for the body. Urging us not to reject the body, she describes it as the *svarūp*, the Self's own form: an opportunity to take bodied human existence seriously as an experiment in perfectibility. Lalla suggests that, by refining away the lower passions, the aspirant can realise the potentiality of the soul's corporal sheath, so that it reveals itself to be 'this body as bright as the sun', *yathi kaṅdi tīz tay sor prakāśa*.

142. K: 25

zanum prāvith vĕbav nō tsōṇḍum

In this brief and intensely moving manifesto, similar in tenor to poems 45 and 90, Lalla asserts that she never sought fame, notoriety or affluence in life; nor did she wish to indulge in the pleasures of the floating world of appearances and desires. The oddly personal detail in the third line, concerning her moderate meals, gathers poignancy when she passes lightly over her years of starvation and pain, to close the poem with the healing vision of the Divine.

143. G: 73

tsāmar chọthar rathu simhāsan

144. G: 74

kyāh bŏḍukh muha bhawa-sŏdari-dārĕ

145. G: 75

karm zah kāran trah kŏmbith

146. G: 76 | K: 102

jñānąki ambar pairith tanĕ

The poems numbered 143, 144, 145 and 146 here form a group of variations on the contrast between absorption in worldly pleasures and absorption in the spiritual question, with the fear of death as a constant presence; indeed, all four poems end with variations on the disquieting phrase, maranūnü shŏkh.

Poem 143 lays out the privileges of royal status: the regalia of the chowry or yak-tail fly-whisk, the ceremonial canopy, the chariot and the lion throne; the enjoyment of theatrical performances, a comfortable bed. But can these withstand the fear of death? Poem 144 is set in the Kashmiri countryside, and pits the fugitive self that has squandered the opportunity for transcendence and fallen into the 'marsh of shadows' against the inexorable figure of Yama, Lord of Death. His warders are unforgiving in the prosecution of their task; in dragging the fugitive to Yama's palace, they subject him, in Lalla's words, to the mediaeval punishment known in Kashmiri as *chōra-dārě karun*, when the prisoner is dragged along the ground, so that he leaves a wake of blood behind him.

In poem 145, Lalla lays out a succinct metaphysics of redemption. There are two kinds of karma: good and bad, each leaving its residues. There are three kinds of causes of the conditional existence of the material world, all technically defined as *malas* or taints: *āṇava-mala*, the taint of believing that the soul is finite; *māyīya-mala*, the taint of maintaining cognitive distinctions between one thing and another; and *kārma-mala*, the taint of generating action, and therefore pleasure and pain. The residues of both kinds of karma and all three taints must be destroyed by the yogini, using the breath-control technique of *kumbhaka*, holding up and containing the body's vital breath currents. The yogini's passage through life must be, in J. Krishnamurti's vivid and memorable phrase, like the flight of the eagle, which leaves no mark. Poem 145 celebrates the soul's journey to the Supreme, transiting through the house of the sun.

In poem 146, the last *vākh* in this translation, Lalla invites the aspirant to put on the robe of wisdom and commit her *vākhs* to memory and practice. Through mindful devotion to the primal syllable, Om, she says, she became absorbed in the light of the awakened consciousness, *tsěth-jyōti*, and so defeated the fear of death: an exemplar that can be emulated, a spiritual technology of hope and liberation that can be passed on to future generations.

References

I. Lal Děd: Translations and Commentaries

Translations

Grierson, Sir George Abraham and Lionel D. Barnett, trans. and eds. 1920. *Lallā-Vākyāni, or the wise sayings of Lal Ded, A mystic poetess of ancient Kashmir*. Vol. 27 of Asiatic Society Monographs. London: The Royal Asiatic Society.

Kak, Jaishree. 2007. *The mystical verses of Lallā*. New Delhi: Motilal Banarsidass.

Kaul, Jayalal. 1973. *Lal Ded*. New Delhi: Sahitya Akademi.

Kotru, Nil Kanth, trans. 1989. *Lal Ded: Her life and sayings*. Srinagar: Utpal Publications.

Lalded Issue. 1971. *Koshur Samāchār: A Socio-cultural Monthly* 9 (1): 1–58.

Parimoo, B.N. 1987. *The ascent of self: A reinterpretation of the mystical poetry of Lalla-Ded*. New Delhi: Motilal Banarsidass.

Temple, Sir Richard Carnac. 1924. *The words of Lalla the prophetess*. Cambridge: Cambridge Univ. Press.

Reworking

Barks, Coleman, trans. 1992. *Naked song*. Athens, GA: Maypop Books.

Studies

Koul, Pandit Ananda. 'Life Sketch of Laleshwari' and 'Lallā-Vākyani'. *The Indian Antiquary*: Vols. 50 (1921): 309–12; 59 (1930): 108–30; 60 (1931): 191–93; 60 (1932): 13–16; 62 (1933): 108–11.

Odin, Jaishree Kak. 1999. *To the other shore: Lalla's life and poetry*. New Delhi: Vitasta Publications.

Toshkhani S.S., ed., 2002. *Lal Ded: The great Kashmiri saint-poetess.* New Delhi: APH Publishing Corporation and Kashmir Education, Culture and Science Society.

Related Sources

Bazaz, P.N. 1959. *Daughters of theVitasta.* New Delhi: Pamposh Publications.

Cook, Nilla Cram. 1958. *The way of the swan: Poems of Kashmir.* Bombay: Asia Publishing House.

Knowles, Rev. J. Hinton. 1985. *A dictionary of Kashmiri proverbs and sayings.* New Delhi: Asian Educational Services. (Orig. pub. 1885.)

Koul, Pandit Ananda. 1933. 'The wise sayings of Nand Rishi'. *The Indian Antiquary* 62.

Parimoo, B.N. 1984. *Nund Rishi: Unity in diversity.* Srinagar: Jammu and Kashmir Academy of Art, Culture and Languages.

II. Kashmir Śaivism and Yoga

Kashmir Śaivism

Avalon, Arthur [Sir John Woodroffe]. 1916. *Principles of Tantra (Tantra Tattva) of Shrīyukta Shiva ChandraVidyārnava Bhattāchārya Mahodaya.* London: Luzac.

———. 1978. *Shakti and Shākta.* NewYork: Dover. (Orig. pub. 1965.)

Deshpande, G.T. 1989. *Abhinavagupta.* New Delhi: Sahitya Akademi.

Dhar,Triloki Nath. 1977. *Rūpa Bhawāni: Life, teachings, and philosophy.* Srinagar: Valley Printing Press.

Dikshitar, V.R. Ramachandra. 1991. *The Lalitā cult.* New Delhi: Motilal Banarsidass.

Drabu, Vishva Nath. 1990. *Śaivāgamas.* New Delhi: Indus Publishing.

Dupuche, John R. 2003. *Abhinavagupta:The Kula ritual.* New Delhi: Motilal Banarsidass.

Dyczkowski, Mark. 1987. *The doctrine of vibration: An analysis of the doctrines and practices of Kashmir Śaivism.* Albany, NY: SUNY Press.

Flood, Gavin. 1993. *Body and cosmology in Kashmir Śaivism*. San Francisco: Mellon Research Univ. Press.

Gnoli, Raniero. 1993. *The aesthetic experience according to Abhinavagupta*. Varanasi: Chowkhamba Sanskrit Series.

Ingalls, Daniel H.H., Jeffrey M. Masson, and M.V. Patwardhan, trans. 1990. *The Dhvanyāloka of Anandavardhana, with the Locana of Abhinavagupta*. Cambridge, Mass.: Harvard Univ. Press.

Kramrisch, Stella. 1981. *The presence of Śiva*. Princeton, NJ: Princeton University Press.

Lakshman Joo, Swami. 1988. *Kashmir Shaivism: The secret supreme*. Albany, NY: SUNY Press.

_____. 2007. *Shiva Sutras: The supreme awakening*. Ed. John Hughes. Bloomington, Indiana: AuthorHouse.

Niranjanananda Saraswati, Swami. 1995. *Yoga Sadhana Panorama*. Vol. 1. Munger: Bihar School of Yoga.

_____. 1997. *Yoga Sadhana Panorama*. Vol. 2. Munger: Bihar School of Yoga.

O'Flaherty, Wendy Doniger. 1973. *Asceticism and eroticism in the mythology of Śiva*. Oxford: Oxford Univ. Press.

Pandit, B.N. 1977. *Aspects of Kashmir Śaivism*. Srinagar: Utpal Publications.

_____. 1990. *History of Kashmir Śaivism*. Srinagar: Utpal Publications.

Pandit, Moti Lal. 2003. *Trika Śaivism of Kashmir*. New Delhi: Munshiram Manoharlal.

Satyananda Saraswati, Swami. 1983. *Meditations from the Tantras*. Munger: Bihar School of Yoga.

Singh, Jaideva, trans. 1979a. *Pratyabhijñāhridayam:The secret of self-recognition*. New Delhi: Motilal Banarsidass.

_____, trans. 1979b. *Śiva Sūtras: The Yoga of supreme identity*. New Delhi: Motilal Banarsidass.

_____. trans. 1979c. *Vijñānabhairava or divine consciousness*. New Delhi: Motilal Banarsidass.

_____, trans. 1980. *Spanda Kārikas*. New Delhi: Motilal Banarsidass.

Vidyāratna, Tārānātha, ed. 1917. *Kulārnava Tantra*. Part V, *Tantrik Texts*, ed. Arthur Avalon [Sir John Woodroffe]. London: Luzac.

Yoga

Baba, Bangali, trans. 1976. *The Yogasūtra of Patañjali*, with the commentary of *Vyāsa*. New Delhi: Motilal Banarsidass.

Eliade, Mircea. 1969. *Yoga: Immortality and freedom*. Trans. Willard R. Trask. Bollingen Series 56. Princeton, NJ: Princeton Univ. Press.

———. 1975. *Patanjali and Yoga*. Trans. Charles Lam Markmann. New York: Schocken Books.

Smart, Ninian. 1996. *Dimensions of the sacred: An anatomy of the world's beliefs*. London: Harper Collins.

Zimmer, Heinrich. *Artistic form and Yoga in the sacred images of India*. Trans. and eds. Gerald Chapple, James B. Lawson and Michael J. McKnight. New Delhi: Oxford Univ. Press.

III. Kashmiri History, Culture, and Society

Bamzai, P.N.K. 1994. *Culture and political history of Kashmir*. Vols. 1–3. New Delhi: M.D. Publications.

Dhar, Somnath. 1977. *Jammu and Kashmir*. New Delhi: National Book Trust.

Goetz, Hermann. 1969. *Studies in the history and art of Kashmir and the Indian Himalaya*. Wiesbaden: Otto Harrassowitz,.

Hasan, Mohibbul. 1959. *Kashmir under the sultans*. Calcutta: Iran Society.

Jonarāja. 2000. *The Rājatarangini of Jonarāja*. Trans. and ed. Jogesh Chunder Dutt. New Delhi: Gyan Publishing House.

Kalhana. 1900. *Rājatarangini: A chronicle of the kings of Kashmir*. Trans. and Ed. Sir Marc Aurel Stein. London: Archibald Constable.

———. 1990. *Rājatarangini*. Trans. Ranjit Sitaram Pandit. New Delhi: Sahitya Akademi.

M.L. Kapoor. 1971. *A history of mediaeval Kashmir*. Jammu: ARB Publications.

Khan, M. Ishaq. 2002. *Kashmir's transition to Islam: The role of Muslim Rishis*. New Delhi: Manohar.

Knowles, Rev. J. Hinton. 2004. *Kashmiri folk tales*. Srinagar: Ali Mohammad and Sons. (Orig. pub. 1893.)

Madan, T.N. 1988. *Non-renunciation: Themes and interpretations of Hindu culture*. New Delhi: Oxford Univ. Press.

———. 1989. *Family and kinship: A study of the Pandits of rural Kashmir*. New Delhi: Oxford Univ. Press.

Pal, Pratapaditya, ed. 1989. *Art and architecture of ancient Kashmir*. Bombay: Marg Publications.

Rafiqi, Abdul Qaiyum. 1972. *Sufism in Kashmir*. Varanasi and New Delhi: Bharatiya Publishing House.

Ray, S.C. 1969. *Early history and culture of Kashmir*. New Delhi: Motilal Banarsidass.

Sikand, Yoginder. 2003. *Sacred spaces: Exploring traditions of shared faith in India*. New Delhi: Penguin Books.

Sufi, G.M.D. 1979. *Islamic Culture in Kashmir*. New Delhi: Light and Life Publishers.

Wani, Muhammad Ashraf. 2005. *Islam in Kashmir (14th to 16th century)*. Srinagar: Oriental Publishing House.

———. 2007. The nature of mass Islamic conversion in Kashmir. *Kashmir Affairs* 2 (2): 13–21.

IV. Kashmiri Language and Literature

Grierson, Sir George Abraham. 1932. *A dictionary of the Kashmiri language*. Calcutta: The Royal Asiatic Society of Bengal.

———. 1969. *The Pisaca languages of north-western India*. New Delhi: Munshiram Manoharlal. (Orig. pub. 1906.)

Handoo, Jawahar Lal. 1973. *Kashmiri phonetic reader*. Mysore: Central Institute of Indian Languages.

Kachru, Braj B. 1969a. Kashmiri and other Dardic languages. In *Current Trends in Linguistics* 5, ed. Thomas A. Sebeok, 284–306. The Hague: Mounton.

————. 1969b. *A reference grammar of Kashmiri*. Urbana: Univ. of Illinois Press.

————. 1981. *Kashmiri literature*. Wiesbaden: Otto Harrassowitz.

Koul, Omkar N. 1977. *Linguistic studies in Kashmiri*. New Delhi: Bahri Publications.

————. 1984. Modes of address in Kashmiri. In *Aspects of Kashmiri Linguistics*, eds. Omkar N. Koul and Peter Edwin Hook, 154–72. New Delhi: Bahri Publications.

Monier Williams, Sir Monier et al. 1920. *A Sanskrit–English dictionary*. Oxford: Oxford Univ. Press.

Ostler, Nicholas. 2005. *Empires of the word: A language history of the world*. London: Harper Perennial.

Palmer, E.H. 2002. *A concise dictionary, together with a simplified grammar, of the Persian language*. New Delhi: Asian Educational Services. (Orig. pub. 1883.)

Platts, John T. 2006. *A dictionary of Urdū, classical Hindī and English*. New Delhi: Manohar.

V. Indian Religion, Philosophy and Culture

Anthologies

Alphonso-Karkala, John B., ed. 1971. *An anthology of Indian literature*. Harmondsworth: Penguin Books.

Gerber, William, ed. 1977. *The mind of India*. Carbondale, IL: Southern Illinois Univ. Press.

Heehs, Peter, ed. 2002. *Indian religions: The spiritual traditions of South Asia*. New Delhi: Permanent Black.

Buddhism

Bucknell, Roderick S. and Martin Stuart-Fox. 1986. *The twilight language: Explorations in Buddhist meditation and symbolism*. London: Curzon Press.

Conze, Edward, ed. 1959. *Buddhist scriptures*. Harmondsworth: Penguin Books.

Easwaran, Eknath, trans. 1987. *The Dhammapada*. Harmondsworth: Penguin Books.

Evans-Wentz, W. Y. and Lobzang Jivaka. 1962. *The life of Milarepa*. New Delhi: Rupa.

Fischer-Schreiber, Ingrid, Franz-Karl Ehrhard and Michael S. Diener, eds. 1991. *The Shambhala dictionary of Buddhism and Zen*. Trans. Michael H. Kohn. Boston: Shambhala.

Skilton, Andrew [Dharmacari Sthiramati]. 1994. *A concise history of Buddhism*. Birmingham: Windhorse.

Bhakti

Chitre, Dilip, trans. 1991. *Tukaram: Says Tuka*. New Delhi: Penguin Books.

———, trans. and ed. 1996. *Śri Jñāneśvara's Anubhavāmrut: The immortal experience of being*. New Delhi: Sahitya Akademi.

Dharwadker, Vinay, trans. 2003. *Kabir: The songs of the weaver*. New Delhi: Penguin Books.

Hess, Linda and Sukhdev Singh, trans. 1986. *The Bijak of Kabir*. New Delhi: Motilal Banarsidass.

Ramanujan, A.K., trans. 1973. *Speaking of Śiva*. Harmondsworth: Penguin Books.

Schomer, Karine. 1987. The Dōhā as a vehicle of Sant teachings. In *The Sants: Studies in a devotional tradition of India*, eds. Karine Schomer and W.H. McLeod, 61–90. New Delhi: Motilal Banarsidass.

Sundaram, P.S., trans. 1996. *The Azhwars: For the love of god*. New Delhi: Penguin Books.

Vaudeville, Charlotte, trans. 1993. *A weaver called Kabir*. New Delhi: Oxford Univ. Press.

Classical Hinduism

Easwaran, Eknath, trans. 1986. *The Bhagavad Gita*. Tomales, CA: Nilgiri Press.

_____, trans. 1996. *The Upanishads*. New Delhi: Penguin Books.

Danielou, Alain. 1964. *The myths and gods of India*. Vermont: Inner Traditions International. (Orig. pub. 1964.)

Hiriyanna, M. 1996. *Essentials of Indian philosophy*. London: Diamond Books.

Sen, K.M. 1961. *Hinduism*. Harmondsworth: Penguin Books.

Zimmer, Heinrich. 1972. *Myths and symbols in Indian art and civilisation*. Ed. Joseph Campbell. Bollingen Series 6. Princeton, NJ: Princeton Univ. Press.

Islam, including Sufism

Attar, Farid ud-Din. 1984. *The conference of the birds*. Trans. Afkham Darbandi and Dick Davis. Harmondsworth: Penguin Books.

Burckhardt, Titus. 1995. *Introduction to Sufism*. Trans. D.M. Matheson. London: Harper Collins.

Dawood, N.J., trans. 2006. *The Koran*. London: Penguin Books.

Manjhan. 2000. *Madhumālatī: An Indian Sufi romance*. Trans. Aditya Behl and Simon Weightman. New York: Oxford Univ. Press.

Schimmel, Annemarie. 1975. *Mystical dimensions of Islam*. Chapel Hill: Univ. of North Carolina Press.

_____. 1982. *As through a veil: Mystical poetry in Islam*. New York: Columbia Univ. Press.

Shah, Idries. 1968. *The way of the Sufi*. Harmondsworth: Penguin Books.

_____. 1971. *The Sufis*. Introduction by Robert Graves. New York: Random House. (Orig. pub. 1964.)

Religion and Culture: General

Campbell, Joseph. 2008. *The hero with a thousand faces*. Novato, CA: New World Library. (Orig. pub. 1968.)

Easwaran, Eknath. 1986. *Meditation: Commonsense directions for an uncommon life*. Harmondsworth: Penguin.

Eliade, Mircea. 1965. *The two and the one*. Trans. J.M. Cohen. Chicago: The Univ. of Chicago Press.

James, William. 1960. *The varieties of religious experience: A study in human nature*. London and Glasgow: Collins.

Lannoy, Richard. 1971. *The speaking tree: A study of Indian culture and society*. Oxford: Oxford Univ. Press.

McEvilley, Thomas. 2008. *The shape of ancient thought: Comparative studies in Greek and Indian philosophies*. New Delhi: Motilal Banarsidass. (Orig. pub. 2002.)

Pachori, Satya S. 1993. *Sir William Jones: A reader*. New Delhi: Oxford University Press.

VI. Anthropology, Political History, Cultural Theory

Anderson, Benedict. 1991. *Imagined communities: Reflections on the origin and spread of nationalism*. London: Verso.

Assmann, Jan. 2006. *Religion and cultural memory: Ten studies*. Trans. Rodney Livingstone. Stanford: Stanford University Press.

Bakhtin, Mikhail M. 1991. *The dialogic imagination: Four essays*. Ed. Michael Holquist. Trans. Caryl Emerson and Michael Holquist. Austin: University of Texas Press.

Cohn, Bernard S. 1988. *An anthropologist among the historians and other essays*. New Delhi: Oxford University Press.

Geertz, Clifford. 1993. *The interpretation of cultures: Selected essays*. London: Fontana Press.

Acknowledgements

I would like to thank my parents, Chandra and Raghuvir Hoskote, for more than I could ever put into words: my life as a writer began with their indulgent and unwavering faith that I would, in fact, be able to make such a life for myself. This book is dedicated to them.

I would also like to thank my wife, Nancy Adajania, for more than two decades of intense companionship and collaborative adventures; and in particular, for her encouragement of my Lalla project and her meticulous responses to this manuscript in its various avatars. This book is a journey we have made together.

Although this is my twentieth book to appear in print, it could very well have been my first. No mystery is intended: I began work on it in February 1991, shortly before putting together my first collection of poems, *Zones of Assault*, which was published later that year. Over these many years, I, *Lalla* has benefited considerably from the pressure exerted by a circle of friends who have charted its progress, and constantly summoned me back to it. Specifically, I wish to thank Shirin, Jehangir and Aafreed Sabavala, who embraced Lalla, asked searching questions, offered responses and periodically demanded results; and Mehlli and Cavas Gobhai, to whose chikoo orchard in Gholvad we have all retreated annually for New Year's, on which occasions these translations have been read and tested out.

There is much that can never adequately be acknowledged. Having admitted this, I record my thanks to four brother writers and fellow pilgrims: Ilija Trojanow, for his passionate belief in the writerly life as a ceaseless experiment in consciousness, his infectious and life-affirming optimism and abundant generosity of spirit; Richard Lannoy, for his intellectual adventurousness and receptivity towards all that seems enigmatic and strange, and his refreshingly original approach to Indian culture and religious life; Jürgen Brôcan, for his love of the travelling text and the spirit of place, his sensitivity to the grammar of the invisible hovering above the page; and Axel Fussi, for conversations on Indic mysticism as a discovery procedure, and for a magical weekend in Ehrwald, where J. Krishnamurti experienced his key process of transformation.

*

My thanks are due to Daniel Weissbort, who directed the Iowa Translation Workshop, University of Iowa, Iowa City, where I first read from these translations and discussed them, in 1995; and to the Librarian and Staff of the University of Iowa Library, the Brown University Library, and the Asiatic Society of Bombay, for their invaluable help in sourcing texts and materials.

For their hospitality and collegiality, I would like to acknowledge my colleagues at five writing residencies which provided me with a most conducive combination of emotional repose and bracing intellectual exchange: in 1995, the International Writing Program at the University of Iowa (Clark Blaise, Daniel Weissbort, Peter and Mary Nazareth, Marc Nieson and Carolyn Brown); in 2003, Villa Waldberta, Munich (Verena Nolte, Karin Sommer, Eva Schuster, and Katrin Dirschwigl); in Spring 2010, Theater der Welt, Essen/Mülheim (Christine Peters,

Frie Lysen and Max Philip Aschenbrenner); in Spring 2010 also, 'The Promised City', mobilised by the Goethe-Institut, Bombay and Warsaw, and the Polnisches Institut, Berlin (Marla Stukenberg, Martin Wälde, Tomasz Dabrowski and Jacek Glaszcz); and in Autumn 2010, BAK/basis voor actuele kunst, Utrecht (Maria Hlavajova, Cosmin Costinas, Arjan van Meeuwen, and Marlies van Hak).

My thanks are due, also, to Nissim Ezekiel, who chose some of these translations for the poetry page that he edited for The Independent (Bombay) in the early 1990s, as well as to Stefan Weidner, Editor, Art and Thought (Bonn), and Bina Sarkar Ellias, Editor, International Gallerie (Bombay), who have published earlier versions of some of these translations.

*

This project has drawn sustenance from the keen interest of Veer Munshi and Gargi Raina: friends from other branches of the Kashmiri diaspora, with whom I have often talked about the complex fate of our homeland. For illuminating and deeply moving conversations in Srinagar, I thank Shafi Shauq, poet, linguist and Head of the Department of Kashmiri, University of Kashmir.

I wish to record a lasting debt of gratitude, also, to my late cousin, Pandit Gurudutt Shukla, for initiating me long ago into an appreciation of the beauty and elegance of my Kashmir Śaiva heritage. He was snatched away too early for me to share fully in his various commitments to philosophy, Hindustani classical music and Sanskrit aesthetics; but he guided me towards the startling epiphany that the Vedanta of Śankara is not the only or the most productive world-view in the

Hindu philosophical universe. That understanding informs the present book.

*

At Penguin, for their kindness, patience, generosity and friendship, which have survived my various delays and numerous missed deadlines, I thank Ravi Singh and R. Sivapriya. Ravi received this idea with his customary warmth and enthusiasm many years ago; as an evolving manuscript, it could not have been placed in more sensitive and meticulous hands than Sivapriya's. I would also like to thank Bhavi Mehta for her exquisite cover design for the original hardcover edition of this book, based on the *kong-poush*, the saffron flower, which evokes both Lalla's profound solitude as well as the gift of her poems, which have crossed great distances in space and time, to enter many hearts.